GIRLS ARE EQUAL TOO

GIRLS ARE EQUAL TOO

The Women's Movement for Teenagers

DALE CARLSON

Decorations by Carol Nicklaus

ATHENEUM 1977 NEW YORK

This Book is Dedicated
To a Free Soul,
My Daughter
Hannah

The major sources for the facts and statistics in this book were: newspapers and magazines, government publications, and books that deal with feminism, the feminist movement, and the lives and thoughts of women.

Published simultaneously in Canada by
McClelland & Stewart, Ltd.
Manufactured in the United States of America
by Halliday Lithograph Corporation
Designed by Nancy Gruber
First Printing July 1973
Second Printing May 1974
Third Printing August 1974
Fourth Printing February 1975
Fifth Printing August 1975
Sixth Printing May 1976
Seventh Printing July 1977

CONTENTS

WHAT YOU CAN DO ABOUT IT

Think Straight   112
What about Boys?   119
What about Work?   125
What about Marriage?   132
The Fight for
 Your Own Survival   140

Suggested Reading   144

Introduction:
The Put-Down

Like every other girl, you have a lot to learn. And some of the lessons aren't easy. The first, and most basic lesson, is learning to be stupid. You may already have discovered this.

Learning to be stupid is hard. It takes years of work on your part, and an exhausting amount of effort on the part of society. All of it intended to make sure that when you grow up, you will know practically nothing. Or at least, a lot less than boys.

Never mind that you get good marks in arithmetic (girls *do* get consistently better marks in school than boys). You will still not be allowed to admit that you can balance a checkbook.

Never mind that you know how to change a tire on a car

(with a good jack, it takes less physical effort to change a tire than to scrub a floor). You will not be allowed to grasp anything so mechanical.

Never mind that you know how to read (which you have probably been doing since you were six). You will still not be allowed to understand the contents of newspapers, books, magazines, or the instructions that come with the washing machine.

Never mind that you will probably have spent twelve, sixteen or more years in school (depending on how long it takes you to learn not to learn). When you apply for a job and want equal pay, interesting challenges, a position that leads to management, someone will look at you as if you were crazy or joking or both.

As I said, it takes a long time to learn that lesson in stupidity.

Which brings us to the second difficult task: learning to be inferior. It is not enough to *know* less than boys, you must *be* less.

Never mind that your intelligence is the same, your ability to work is the same (*plus* you can have a baby if you want to). You will not be allowed even to hint at your equality, much less any superiority.

Never mind that girls have greater endurance (we sustain activity, cold, fatigue, longer; we even live longer). You are still the weaker sex.

Never mind that you were born with greater verbal, perceptual, and analytical skills than boys (which means that if girls were brought up the same as boys, girls would be in a better position to cope with the world than boys are). You are still not fit to make decisions or be a leader.

Never mind that it doesn't make sense to be inferior. Just hang your head and stand there.

The third lesson girls have to learn is how to be passive. From the beginning of their lives, boys are brought up to go out and do something and reap the rewards. What girls are brought up to do is stand around and watch.

You're good at sports and you'd like to be on a team? Forget it. Be a cheerleader, and let the boys do the winning.

You have an aptitude for biology? Fine, but be a nurse, not a doctor. That way, you won't compete too much, and you'll have lots of chances to clap for the doctor. (The same rule holds for any field. Interested in law or government? Be a legal secretary. Don't, heaven forbid, be a lawyer or run for office yourself. Good at writing or art? Don't do it, teach it. Have a bent for science? Avoid the creative aspects of research and be a lab technician.)

While it's perfectly true that you have excellent legs for standing or running on and an able mind to think with, avoid using them at all costs. Use only the hands, to clap with. And when you get tired of clapping for your boyfriend or eventually your husband, don't worry. You can always have sons and clap for them. (Not your daughters, however. Remember, they, too, have to learn to be stupid, inferior, and passive.)

Passivity, of course, leads neatly into the fourth necessity for a girl. Dependence. A really *good* girl is not just passive, she takes it one step farther. She *leans* a little.

You may be able to cope with your homework, form a political opinion, even get and hold a job. But you shouldn't, at least not without getting lots of advice and help. It makes people happy to think of you as a helpless child.

It's even better, of course, if you bungle your work and can't begin to form an opinion of your own. You'll lose everybody's respect and your self-respect along with it. But you'll find everybody thinks you're as adorable as a pet poodle.

And that brings us to an extremely important matter, being adorable. A truly feminine girl has to be beautiful at all times.

You're not all that frantically interested in clothes and

makeup? It doesn't matter. You'll always be daddy's little darling even if everyone else thinks you're a dog.

You have weird legs and a crooked nose? That's all right. All the models on television had problems like yours until they Clairoled themselves blonds.

You've tried every kind of makeup, three hairdos, low heels, high heels, miniskirts, maxiskirts, pants, loose shirts, tight sweaters, and you still don't look like a movie actress? Try again. Go on trying until you die trying. Men don't have to be beautiful, but you do!

Then there's the game of "even if I win, I lose." This is related to your general knowledge of your own inferiority.

Even if you could pick him up and throw him across the gym, he's stronger.

Even if you're into advanced calculus or get straight A's (supposing that you haven't quite mastered the lesson of stupidity), and he's still struggling with last year's spelling test—he's smarter.

Even if you have to walk on your knees to date him, remember, he's taller.

Even if everybody wants you for class president, bribe them not to vote for you against a boy. You're supposed to serve men, not lead them. Avoid all success like the plague!

(This will, of course, frustrate you terribly. And you won't EVER get used to it. But somebody will be there to pay the bills when you gnash your teeth to the nerves, get terrible stomach cramps, are knocked flat with a migraine headache, or need psychiatric help. Somebody else will have to pay the bills—you'll never be allowed to be successful enough to pay them yourself.)

And speaking of FRUSTRATION—well, we've hardly begun. Besides being expected to play with dolls and tea sets while boys can explore the real world of rocks and fields and city streets, and having to keep your pretty pink dress clean while boys can wear anything they want and get it dirty, and being allowed to play a little jacks while boys run and throw balls and really develop their bodies—besides all that, you're supposed to be NICE about it.

If a boy punched you in the stomach, did anybody approve of you if you punched him back? Of course not. Nice girls are gentle.

If a brother or sister took your toys or borrowed your possessions without asking, did people approve if you made a loud noise about it? Of course not. Nice girls are kind, giving, and above all, QUIET.

And how about the times you came home late for supper, left your room in a mess, forgot to do your homework, got dirty, had a fight, disobeyed someone's orders? Hah! Boys will be boys, but girls must be obedient, clean, and ladylike at all times.

Of course, if you insisted on climbing trees, playing baseball, having adventures, and wearing an old pair of pants everyday, you were called a tomboy. Maybe, up to a point, everybody even thought it was cute. But that foolishness is supposed to straighten out when you finally realize, sometimes as early as seven or eight, sometimes not until your mid-teens, your true function in life.

Your true function in life—have you figured out what that is yet? Have you properly understood what the whole put-down is really leading up to? The bringing up (or, rather, bringing down) of most girls qualifies them to become, not mature, intelligent adults with the right to call their souls and dreams their own, but only part of that vast, domestic army that nurtures, supports, takes care of everybody else. The function is called *housewife*.

The point is, that while a boy learns he can be a husband, a father, and a doctor, lawyer, or the president of the United States, a girl learns she can be a wife and a mother, period.

(You're allowed, of course, to get a job or think about a career, but nobody takes it too seriously the way they take men's
work, right? I mean, after all, you're just going to get married
and have babies anyway.)

Another point is, that while boys are brought up to please
other people some of the time and please themselves some of
the time (that's called setting up one's own standards, initiative,
creativity, masculinity, aggressiveness), you are brought up to
please other people—first your parents, then your teachers,
then boys, then your husband, and then, so you don't get out
of practice, your children. And you're supposed to please them
all of the time. (That's called charm.) The reason for charm
is so that when you find yourself doing dishes, scrubbing floors,
changing diapers, and all those other mindless, boring, repeti-
tive tasks, you will always seem to be happy. A smiling, happy
slave produces less guilt in everyone else than a cranky one.
Then you will not just be a housewife, but a *happy housewife,*
which pleases everyone enormously.

Do you finally understand what is being done to you just
because you are a girl? A system that divides up what girls are
allowed to do from what boys are allowed to do or makes rules
for how girls have to behave and how boys have to behave is
called a sex-role system. Or just sexism. The role you play in
life, says a sexist society, is determined not by your own
unique individuality, your own talents and ambitions, but by
whether you happen to be a male or a female. A sexist society
says a female is less intelligent, inferior, and has to learn to be
passive, dependent, gentle, obedient, supportive, motherly; and
a boy is more intelligent, superior, and has to learn to be
active, independent, aggressive, brave, competitive, successful.
A sexist society brings up its girls to have babies and do housework and take lower-paying jobs, work it calls less important,
inferior to the work boys will do. A sexist society insists that
the physical difference between being male and female (which

makes a difference only in making love and making babies) should also prevent half the human race from developing in areas that have nothing whatever to do with sex.

The women's-liberation movement, feminism, represents women's battle against sexism and all it stands for. The struggle is against unequal pay, discrimination in educational and job opportunities, and the unfair legal restrictions on women's rights. The struggle is for day-care centers where children can be well taken care of while women work. The struggle is against sexist upbringing, which is as unfair to boys, by forcing them to live up to ideals of masculinity, as it is to girls in forcing them to live up to ideals of femininity. But mostly, women's liberation is a battle against the enforced making of every woman into a wife, a mother, a housekeeper, and a second-class citizen.

Tired of being inferior? Read on.

Section One

THE WAY IT IS

Growing Up a Girl

From the beginning it goes wrong. Even in the hospital nursery—which should be full of baby human beings, *all* of whom have the potential to grow into something special—they've already started handing the ribbons out. Pink for you, blue for the kid in the next bassinet.

Now there's nothing wrong with pink. Basically, it's a perfectly all right color. But eventually, when you go to trade in a pink ribbon, what you get for it every time is a set of dishes, two dozen diapers, and a vacuum cleaner. (With a blue ribbon, you get choices—a spaceship, a shortstop mitt, a seat in Congress.) And if you're listening to the conversations when they bring you home to your cradle, what you hear if you're a

boy is, "Wonder what he's going to do when he grows up?" Not
if you're a girl, though, lying there clutching your pink ribbon.
What they say about you is, "She'll be such a beautiful bride."
The crucial point is made right from the moment of birth.

If you are a boy, you're going to go out into the world and
do something; you will learn independence, grow into maturity,
and find your identity through your work.

If you are a girl, you won't actually *do* anything. You'll go
on being a girl, and sooner or later, nature will take its course,
and some nice man will come along and take care of you.

The sex roles have been handed out. A boy has to do and do
and do to constantly prove his masculinity. And a girl isn't
allowed to do anything much or she will disprove her femininity. It isn't really fair to either sex. Although even if it's
rougher on the boys to begin with, it pays off later. Because at
least boys can choose their destiny; the destiny of girls is always
the same. Pick up a mop, have a baby, and join the parade.

Training begins early. It has to. Contrary to the fact that for
thousands of years people have thought that girls were born
intellectually inferior to boys, studies have shown that there
are no innate intellectual differences between boys and girls.
So, society, while it encourages a boy to grow, has to put a lot
of pressure on a girl to keep her from growing. It isn't easy.
Human beings, all human beings, have a need to grow that is
just as basic to their nature as eating and sleeping. But there
you are, you're a girl, and you have to be trimmed down to size.

In infancy and the early childhood years, psychologists have
noted that boys are more physically active and aggressive than
girls, while girls have greater verbal skills and a better understanding of their environment. This means that boys are what
society calls "naughtier" than girls, and girls, because of their
early understanding of what is expected of them, learn the
pleasure of having other people's approval. One result of this
is that by the time children are four or five, a boy has already
learned to look to himself for approval, to develop a sense of

self in the outer, real world, to value himself in terms of his own achievement rather than through somebody else's approval. A girl is never forced into this position. All she has to do, which she can do very well because of her lesser aggression and her excellent analytical skills, is to conform to what is expected of her and go on being everybody's darling, lovable little lady.

There is another important factor among these early parental attitudes toward young children. Although all infants and toddlers are dependent, boys are taught early not to cry, not to lean, to stand on their own two feet. Not girls, though. Our dependency is encouraged and rewarded. The lessons in sex roles are learned from the beginning. Boys are pressured to be active, to give up their childish ways, to earn their masculinity, to seek a sense of self in relation to the world. Girls are not pressured to prove anything. They are girls, and that is enough. Because of their ability to learn how to please and the rewards they get for pleasing others, they remain forever dependent on other people's values instead of forming their own. There's Mommy's good girl!

Okay. Now that you've been taught to lean on other people's approval instead of developing your own self-esteem and your own values, what are you being taught and how?

One of the ways children are taught who they are and what they are supposed to do is through the kinds of activities they are given, or applauded for, or scolded for.

Boys are expected to run, jump, explore, climb, fight, get dirty, and take chances with their physical safety.

Ever heard fathers on the subject of their sons?

"Youngest kid on the block, and he can lick them all."

"Fell off his bike three times, but he never stopped trying. Didn't cry, either."

"Dirty? (Chuckle.) You never saw a kid so dirty. Took us a week to get him clean again."

Girls, on the other hand, are expected to be ladies. That includes sitting still as much as possible, being pretty, staying clean, and taking an interest in hanging out the wash, diapering the new baby, or baking a batch of cookies.

Ever heard mothers on the subject of their daughters?

"I tell you, her brownies are better than mine."

"Cute? There she was with her little dust rag, following me around the house."

"She was so proud of how pretty she looked in her new party dress, she didn't get a speck of dirt on it."

What all this accomplishes is twofold: it teaches a girl her place (behind a mop) and gives her an image (gorgeous). If this is kept up long enough, a girl will grow up to be that perfect specimen—a beautiful domestic servant. What else happens is that already her intellect is being damaged. The ability to cope and the capacity to think through problems are developed when children are allowed to solve things for themselves. Girls are so much more restricted than boys, that they do not learn as early as boys, if ever, to cope with the world.

Children also learn about themselves through the toys they are given to play with. There he is with his football, his chemistry set, his building blocks, his trains, cars, and planes (he, after all, can choose to be a Joe Namath, an Einstein, an architect, a railroad conductor, a test pilot); and there you are with your dolls, dishes, a miniature broom (not much choice of a future there). I don't say that here and there little girls aren't given baseball gloves. But how many hours does Daddy spend burning those fast balls into his little girl's glove compared to the hours he spends with her brother? And I don't say that now and then a little boy doesn't go to a tea party. But have you ever heard his father brag about it at the poker table?

No matter how you look at it, boys are trained early to develop healthy egos and adventurous spirits, while girls are trained to be passive, dependent, obedient, to curb their interests, and stay at home.

Interests. Now there's a good word. All children are born

curious about everything. But that doesn't last very long. By the time girls are two or three, certainly no later than six or seven, they are generally told very specifically what they are and are not interested in. Boys are interested in how frogs jump, how engines run, how electricity works, where the North Pole is. But girls are not going to be scientists, engineers, or explorers. (You've even heard your mother take pride in explaining how unmechanical she is.) Girls are supposed to be far more interested in how to clean the house with the new vacuum cleaner (never mind how it works).

The end of it all, of course, is that having been convinced that you have no interest in the real, outside world of doing and building and working, you are then told that, because you have no such interests, you are somehow inferior and not very bright. This doesn't matter, naturally, because you are pretty and will one day marry a bright, superior man. It's enough to make you scream, if you think about it long enough.

But we haven't finished with the arsenal yet. Other heavy guns are rolled out to keep you in your place. Think about the stories you were told when you were little. In most of them the boys were self-reliant achievers, with goals and a life of their own. Not the girls. The girls were childish, helpless little things whose only reward and safety lay in marriage.

Take *Snow White* as an example. Life with her stepmother was no bed of roses, granted. But does she take off, as a boy would have done, to build herself a house somewhere and try her hand at some berry picking or a little farming? Not Snow White. She hangs around complaining a lot until the huntsman explains he's been ordered to kill her and she better get out in a hurry. Now does she stomp over the nearest horizon to seek her fortune? Don't be silly. She races hysterically into the woods looking for a new domestic setup. She finds one all right. It's perfect for a feminine little girl. Not one, but seven men to wash, dust, and cook for. Does she ever say, "Wouldn't it be fun if I helped with the mining?" Never. But oh, those pies she cooks. And after all her troubles, what's her reward in the end. A conquest? An achievement? An interesting life? Of course not. The man with the biggest palace in the neighborhood, with enough housework to keep her busy the rest of her life. (Compare this to the fun Robin Hood had, or King Arthur's knights, or Puss in Boots.)

And then there's television. Television tells you a lot about the roles of men and women. On television, it's mostly men who run around and do things. Women either wait for the men to come home, or if they're really clever, they help the men out a little. But it's the commercials that really get you. Boys are shown with spaceships, cars, or exciting games that imitate the adult working world. Or else they are shown running around and exercising their bodies. Girls are shown with dolls that need a million dresses (to look gorgeous). Or with their hair being cream rinsed (to look gorgeous). (Do let me remind you that gorgeous is not a career no matter what anybody tells you.) Or else they are helping their mothers with the housework. (Let me also remind you that while housework has to be done, it is not stimulating, and it is definitely not enough to keep you going for a lifetime.) Or else they are shown playing mother to baby dolls. (Babies are fun, they are stimulating, but when they grow up and go away, you still have half your life to live.)

You have not even entered first grade yet (no point in discussing nursery school and kindergarten where, like at home, in books, on television, there are boy things to do and girl things to do), and already you have begun to appreciate the fact that you are not being brought up, as a boy is, to be a husband, father, and something more. You are being brought up to be a wife and mother, period. You are not being brought up to be a complete human being who uses herself to the fullest of her capacities. You are brought up to serve other human beings and to deny a lot of your own potential.

So far, it's been murder. But wait till you get to school.

Girls in School

Everybody knows that the older girls get, the dumber they get. In grammar school, girls get much better marks than boys in all subjects, including arithmetic and science. In junior high school, girls do less well, especially in math and the sciences ("boy stuff," right?); in high school, most girls' marks have dropped markedly (though the level is still higher than boys' marks in most subjects); and by the time girls get to college, many of them have practically given up trying.

Why?

Why does the girl child, who matures so quickly, who starts out so bright, suddenly stop growing mentally, and not only stop, but go backward? Why, oh why, when we were winning the race in the fifth grade, did so many of us suddenly slow down in the seventh, and then by the tenth grade decide to stop running altogether?

Does our intelligence fail? No.

Do we suddenly, in the bloom of our youth, get tired? Not likely.

Are they putting something in our food? Doubtful. (Although sometimes it does seem like a slow poison.)

What's being poisoned is not our minds or our bodies, but our will to succeed. Little by little, we are taught to be afraid of success. We are taught not to compete. We are taught not to be aggressive. The reason? If you are successful, competitive, and aggressive, you are told, boys won't like you.

(This is nonsense. Interesting boys like interesting girls.)

The real difficulty is that it is the need to succeed that sharpens and encourages intelligence; it is the need to achieve that makes people work hard and well. What happens to girls is that, after the early years of grammar school, society takes away the normal need to compete, the normal aggressiveness of every human being, the normal need to succeed, and replaces all of this by giving girls to understand that they would be better off—more *feminine*—if they failed, or at least if they did a lot less well than boys. It is not only sad, it's a crime.

I once heard a ninth-grade girl say wistfully to a friend, "I used to want to be a scientist. I got pretty good marks in science, too. But then my mother said boys don't like girls who are too brainy, so I don't study so much anymore, and my marks have dropped."

Her friend nodded in understanding. "My mother says men don't like it if you do anything too well. She says men like to win all the time, and if you want a husband, you have to learn how to lose. It isn't fair. I *hate* losing just as much as they do."

Many psychologists (mostly men), including Freud, have said that there is something missing in girls that boys have. They have said we lack the same intelligence, the same drive, the same ambition, and that these lacks are what make girls unable to work well, to compete well, to accomplish important things. It is these lacks that make us inferior to men, that make us second-class citizens.

The truth is, girls don't *lack* anything, not intelligence, not ability, not drive. We are simply told to forget about them. We are told to forget about them by the men who like to go on pretending they are superior and by the women who are brainwashed into helping the men pretend.

Remember, when you were in the first, second, third grades, even beyond, how it was all right to be smart? It was easy then. Nobody bothered you then about competing with boys. (At home, of course, you were already role playing; you helped with the dishes while your brother learned to farm, repair the toaster, or recite the names of football heroes.) But at school, even though you sewed while he took shop, and you didn't always play the same games in gym, at least nobody bothered your head. Both sexes were rewarded for academic achievement. (Although recently I came across a professional guide to teaching reading called *Alpha One,* which was so sexist I couldn't believe it. Enough to make any girl child cringe, it told the teacher to give each letter a personality. The vowels, says the text, are five girls who are always crying and complaining about the work they have to do. It's their way of getting sympathy from the boys who are consonants. The text goes on and on and gets worse and worse.)

But girls are set up to do very well in school. At home, they've already learned to depend on other people's approval rather than self-esteem (now they get teacher's approval for sitting still as well as mommy's); they've learned to conform (sit still if everybody else is sitting still); obey (enjoy getting pats on the head for sitting still); and be passive (sit still so they won't get dirty, won't be noisy, won't be unfeminine, etc.). As it happens, this works out very well. You have to be able to sit still if somebody is going to teach you anything at all.

It also happens that with the extra maturity girls have, the better verbal skills and perceptual skills, they learn admirably well what they are expected to learn. And grammar schools are still very feminine institutions where the teachers, most of whom are women, value exactly what little girls are all about.

Your brothers at this point were too twitchy (they ran around too much), too aggressive (they talked back), and too independent (they cared more about objective achievements like winning a race than the approval of grownups and good marks).

So you did well in grammar school. In the area of academic achievement, you were not only allowed to be competitive, aggressive, and successful, you were rewarded for it. Even in athletics at this point in your life, nobody bothered you if you ran faster, climbed higher, or threw a better baseball. By the time you were in the sixth grade, you were probably feeling pretty cocky. You could try hard and be rewarded by success. You felt you could cope with the world and enjoy it, as a person and a girl.

Then all of a sudden something changed. You started looking like a woman instead of a little girl. And with that everybody's mind about you and how you were supposed to behave changed, too. Suddenly, you were no longer a regular person doing her best. You were a female, and you weren't supposed to do too well anymore.

Sexism, role playing according to which sex you are, had begun to interfere with your natural abilities, your natural competitiveness, your natural pleasure in success.

You're interested in boys now (and even if you're not yet all that interested, everybody tells you you should be). And what is the advice you are given? Is it:

"Boys are marvelous creatures, some day you may even want to marry one of them, but in the meantime remember you are a human being first and human beings need to grow and be as successful as their abilities will allow them"?

Never!

The advice you are given, if not openly, by general social pressure, is, "Slow down, cookie. Boys don't want any competition from you. All you have to be from here on in is sexy enough to catch one of them. Never mind the books now, the good marks, the basketball practice. Concentrate on makeup, miniskirts, and man-catching facial expressions."

Now you'd think any self-respecting girl would blink a couple of times in surprise, give a couple of hoots of laughter, and go on with whatever she was doing. (Switch it around and imagine telling a thirteen- or fourteen-year-old boy to give up his chemistry set or his baseball glove in order to concentrate on his clothes so he could catch a wife.) But girls don't laugh the advice and pressures away to go on with whatever they are doing. They listen and obey.

The reason they listen is because they have not been given enough self-respect, because they have had all that early training in dependency on other people's approval. They start out by being trained to need mommy's approval; after that, they achieve well in grade school because of the rewards for this "good" behavior that comes from others (rather than for achievement's own sake). Now society says, "Stop competing if you want approval." So, in order to be approved of, girls stop competing.

The result is that while boys grow more and more afraid of failing (boys have other problems, but this book is about girls), girls grow more and more afraid of succeeding. And without personal success, there is no self-image. Therefore, girls go on depending on others rather than themselves for a sense of worth.

Not only at home and in society does this happen. It even happens in school, which is the one place all people should be given the chance to develop themselves to their fullest capacities.

But both in courses and in counseling, girls get the short end of the stick.

By junior high and high school, you can forget about gym. Even if you haven't been separated from boys before, you're separated then. The excuse is that boys are faster, stronger, and that girls aren't good enough to compete with them. Even if we accept that (although in any class, *some* girls are better athletes than *some* boys), how come girls aren't equally encouraged to develop their bodies? Most of the time it's the boys' team and the boys' sports that everybody claps for, not the girls'.

But the courses are the worst. Why do the boys get shop, printing, woodworking, machines (lots of women work in factories, enjoy woodworking, go into the publishing business), while the girls end up with cooking, sewing, child-care classes? The schools just seem to assume that all boys have more talent for electronics, mechanical drawing, machine parts (not true; girls' aptitudes have been tested and are just as good as boys'); and that all girls are just fascinated with chocolate pudding, needlepoint, and diapering doll bottoms (false!). It's all part of the plot to keep you in your place.

In regular courses, math, the sciences, government, economics, social studies are supposed to be boy stuff. (If you are interested in these things, better not make a point of it, and if you know the answers in class, have the grace to be meek about it in front of the boys.) It's all right, however, to be interested in English literature and the arts. This is feminine stuff (and Lord help the boy who happens to be talented in oil painting, ballet dancing, or writing poetry).

Obviously, this is all ridiculous. Talents and abilities have nothing to do with sex; people of either sex can be capable in almost any area of work and study, but anyone's ability can be murdered by neglect or downright disapproval.

With the courses you take, comes the counseling. The major attitude seems to be, not that you are a human being with

a definite talent or interest (you may have been brainwashed
out of this by now anyway) but that you are a lady and ladies
are supposed to do ladylike work (until you get married when
you will be sent to the kitchen where all nice ladies belong).
What you will find out is that ladylike work, the nursing and
teaching professions, secretarial work and the like, are often
the lowest-paying of all jobs.

Not that there is anything wrong with being a teacher or a
nurse or a secretary. They are all honorable, gratifying,
and most necessary professions. The thing is, though, you
aren't given much choice. Everybody encourages girls to go
into the "mothering" professions (same old role), and there is
very little encouragement for the girl who wants to be a doctor,
a lawyer, a scientist.

And if you like working with your hands or fixing things, nobody says to you, "be a carpenter, or open your own garage."
They tell you to take up knitting or teach arts and crafts.

So when you hear that you are dumber than a boy, less am-
bitious than a boy, inferior in sports or in class, you can just
tell them that if they hadn't hung all that femininity around
your neck, you might have outraced any boy on your block.

Girls and Boys

In spite of the problems (everybody has problems), it's nice to be a girl. And one of the nicest feelings, if you are a girl, is to be with a boy you like and who likes you.

But don't you sometimes wish the relationship between you and boys could be a little more natural, a little less fixed in its rules about who has to do and say what, a little more *human?*

Take a quick look at the dating process. What happens?

Weeks before you even get to the point of an actual date, you have spent a lot of time trying to look adorable. (He has been trying to impress you by making the football team, getting the lead in the school play, or being elected president of his class—which means that even if he doesn't get *you,* he will have achieved something anyway.) If you don't get him, all you'll be left with is a new miniskirt, an extra sweater, and a crushed ego. But since you're not supposed to compete and achieve anything or you'll scare him off, you're left with looking adorable. Looking adorable and hanging around, that is.

Because heaven forbid you should make the first move. You like him, you make a pretty shrewd guess he likes you, but there is absolutely nothing you can do but wait. Even if he's shy and even if you're not, you have to wait for him to do the asking. (If you don't, if *you* ask *him,* maybe people will say you're chasing him, or setting a trap for him. Why? All you want to do is maybe take a walk or go to a movie, not cook him for dinner.)

All right. You have followed rules one and two—looking gorgeous and waiting around—and you have finally batted your eyelashes enough to attract his attention, and he asks you to that movie. The next rule is that he has to pick you up at your house. Even if the movie is nearer his house. Even if you have a car, and he doesn't. Even if he doesn't have much money, and the extra carfare hurts. (The boy-picks-up-the-girl rule is less rigid than it used to be in some communities, but a lot of people still consider it uncouth for a girl to pick up a boy, or for a girl to pay taxi or bus fare.)

Which brings us to the subject of who pays, for the carfare, for the movie, for the restaurant check. You may have more money that week or in general or at least enough money to split expenses. No matter. He's the boy, and he pays. (There are several psychologically damaging things about this rule besides the fact that it isn't fair for the boys to have to spend their money all the time. The boys, who pay, get to feeling an edge of superiority—people who control the money arrangements always do—and girls end up with the feeling they've been bought and paid for and they'd better be nice, a distinctly inferior and childlike position to be stuck in.) Also, because he's paying, you have to go along with what he wants to do, generally, not what you might like to do. (Just out of curiosity, how many times have you kissed a boy because he spent so much money on you that evening? Would you have kissed him if you had paid for the evening?)

So far you've obeyed all the rules of femininity, and he's obeyed all the rules of masculinity (no matter what your true needs as human beings). Now how does the evening go?

He, being the masculine one, leads the way. He may do all the talking, or he may expect you to entertain him. The choice is not usually yours, it's his. If he has opinions on any subject, he will expect you to accept most of them (he's smarter, and anyway you're not supposed to compete with him). You're also supposed to flatter him (mother told you to build up a man's ego) in as many ways as possible. (This is called being feminine.) Other ways to be feminine are to giggle at his jokes, to behave as if you couldn't cross a street by yourself, and to be built like Raquel Welch. (He, if he is properly masculine, will have the grace to be at least six feet tall, be able to lift twice his own weight, and will be planning to be as rich as you are beautiful.)

If you're going to a party, what do you want to bet the girls will get to cope with the food (you're good at details like that), and the boys will sit around talking to each other the way they almost never talk to you (real conversation can only be carried on among men).

If you've got a long-term relationship going, how much time do you spend following him and his friends around compared to the time he spends following you and your friends around? And how much time do you spend clapping for him compared to the clapping he does for you? Of course, he thinks you're pretty. But what else? While you tell him he's a marvelous basketball player (mechanic, guitarist, all-around-hero) what does he tell you? That you write brilliant compositions, quadratic equations, lab reports? Or are you the one who cooks fine, sews a fantastic button, and because you are so nice to him will someday be a terrific mother.

And speaking of your futures, how do you speak of your futures? He's going to be what—an electrician, a lawyer, a businessman, a politician? You take it seriously and encourage him. But you tell him you're going to have a career, and unless it's nursing, teaching, or maybe fashion-designing, you'll see on his face anything from mild shock to hilarity. Jobs are okay, to help out or fill time until you get married, but a serious commitment to a serious ambition? That makes him nervous. Marriage and maternity and wearing pretty clothes should be enough for you. (Ask him sometime if being a husband and a father and a new pair of jeans would be enough for him.)

The funny thing is that there are boys who really do like cooking and child rearing, who might well make excellent housekeepers. But they are too hung up on their masculinity to admit it, and besides, everyone would call them sissies. You may swing a microscope better, and he may sing a better lullaby, but unfortunately each of you is stuck in the machinery of sexism. It just isn't human, any of it.

The two saddest results of the double-sex standard are that: one, girls are too often kept from useful work and from fulfilling themselves as people as well as wives and mothers; and, two, the relationship between boys and girls becomes very difficult, especially for girls. Because a boy is taught that he is strong, aggressive, and the leader, and a girl is weaker, passive, and the follower; because they both learn that his work is more important than her work, that he controls the money while she waits for handouts; because of all this, they both learn quickly that a girl is inferior to a boy.

What this leads to, of course, is that since you aren't his equal, the two of you can't really be friends. Therefore, sex usually forms the only basis of the relationship between you. This gives a lot of girls the sneaking feeling they're being used instead of enjoyed as people. It also means that if you aren't in love with a boy, or he isn't mad about you, it's very hard just to be friends. And when boys get to the point where girls only mean sex, you can hardly get down the street or through the school halls without whistles, catcalls, or remarks. Being attractive is lovely. Being pestered to death is annoying.

Aside from the big problems caused by having to be feminine, how about the small ones? What is all that business about girls are more girlish if they sit a certain way, light a match a certain way, blow it out a certain way, drink a glass of water a certain way (I've talked to some kids who give each other "feminine" and "masculine" tests), wait for doors to be opened, wear skirts instead of pants, frilly blouses, higher heels, and on and on and on. Why should it all matter so much? A more important question is, how do girls get this way? Why do they put up with it all?

The answer is that a part of you enjoys it. (People never do anything for very long unless it satisfies *something* inside them.) Part of you enjoys being small and weak while he is big and strong, part of you enjoys being the follower behind his leadership, part of you enjoys the fact that he is supposed to know much more about the world than you do, part of you even enjoys being put in your place, being inferior. (Think about this; sadly, it's true.)

There are reasons why part of you enjoys it. Sometime around the beginning of adolescence you were told that the only true reward in life for a woman was catching and marrying a man, and that being "feminine" was the only way to get one. So by behaving in this feminine way, you get two gold stars: you get the man, and you get everybody's approval for having gotten him. When you know you're behaving in a way that everybody is going to applaud, your need for approval (because you're a girl) is going to make you enjoy behaving in such a way.

(What nobody ever tells you is that grownups get married

because it's a nice way to live for both men and women, that it happens naturally, that you don't have to work so hard to make sure it happens.)

Another reason girls accept an inferior position to boys is that they *need* boys so badly. Girls, as we have seen, learn to value themselves *only* if other people love and value them. In the beginning a little girl looks to her parents for approval and love, then she looks to her teachers; eventually, as she grows up, she transfers her need for approval to boys. Most girls never learn to look to themselves, to rely on their own achievements to make them feel important. So girls go on playing up to boys because they can't afford to lose their only source of love. They have little self-love to go on.

Feeling inferior to boys is another reason girls put up with being *treated* as inferiors. If you're not encouraged to learn, after a while you're going to stop bothering. And if you stop bothering, you end up nowhere, being treated as if you were nobody.

Being nobody is a terrible problem. But if your whole life is spent playing the role of "girl" how are you going to find out who you really are as a person, what you like and what you don't like, what you're good at and what you're not, what you think and what you don't think? How often have you heard that a man is a girl's destiny, that you're supposed to wait until he hands you your future? He'll become a somebody, and you'll end up as Mrs. Carpenter, or Mrs. Astronaut, or Mrs. Storeowner.

And believe me, being Mrs. Somebody is not the same as being somebody yourself. There's not much sense of personal identity in it and not much pride.

I'm not saying it isn't wonderful to be pretty and attractive and loved. I'm not even saying that every girl should go out and conquer the world.

What I am saying is that being attractive and loved isn't enough to make anybody happy forever, boy or girl, and that everybody, not just boys, should be allowed the pride and sense of identity that comes with knowing how to earn a living at work one chooses to do, at being treated as an adult human being.

The thing is, if girls stopped playing dumb, there wouldn't be anybody left to make the boys feel smarter!

Women in College

You will notice from the chapter title that the word "women" is used, not "girls." If you are old enough to get a job without parent-signed working papers, old enough to get married without parental permission, able enough to be responsible for yourself, you are entitled to be called a woman, not a girl. (If you hear your mother and her friends, or the women of community organizations and card clubs, still referring to themselves as "girls," it is because they have gotten so little satisfaction or reward from maturity. They continue to strain backward toward the only triumphant time of their lives, those girlish years when they caught and married a man. Their image of themselves is still dependent and childlike; they still stand on their husband's feet instead of on their own.)

One of the most important moments in your life comes when you graduate from high school. Will you simply latch onto the nearest man as soon as possible and depend on him to provide you with your future? (Not entirely fair to a man, since it leaves him totally responsible for two and then more lives. And quite possibly dangerous for you, since a man can get sick, or die, or eventually want a divorce. Or even if none of these things happen, you simply can't expect another human being to fill fifty or sixty years of your life with joy. You're going to have to manage to find some satisfaction on your own.

Nobody says it's easy. If, as a girl, you've had it rough in high school with "feminine" courses, bad counseling, and playing second fiddle to the boys, as a woman looking for work or a woman who wants higher education, you're going to find it even rougher.

We haven't discussed the special problems of being black, because up until now the problems have been much the same for all girls, black and white. From here on in, if you happen to be black as well as a woman, you can just about double the difficulties. You have to work against two handicaps: racism and sexism. You have two battles to fight: the first is alongside the black man for racial equality; and the second battle, to be fought alongside sisters of all colors, is against five thousand years of political and psychic oppression of women. (Anthropological studies note that there have been a number of primitive societies where inheritance is matrilineal and where women had status. Among the American Hopi Indians of the Arizona desert, women are almost dominant. Alas, this has never happened in a major civilization, however, so while it proves that the ability to rule is not an inherent characteristic of the male, we still haven't had a real chance at it.)

If you've managed to survive high school without trading in your pink ribbon for a vacuum cleaner (or even if you've got the vacuum cleaner and you're still bent on a larger life), you're going to have to work even harder to survive college with your head in one piece. You're even going to have to work to get into college.

More women finish high school than men. More women get high school academic honors than men. Half the smartest people in our country, half the most talented people in our country, are women. And yet only 40 percent of our college undergraduates are women.

Getting into college is harder for women than for men. Women need higher grades for admission to many colleges and universities. Official and unofficial quota systems for women are widespread. The University of North Carolina at Chapel Hill openly states that "admission of women on the freshman level will be restricted to those who are especially well qualified." And indeed, in the 1969 freshman class, there were 1,893 men and only 426 women. At the University of Michigan for the past ten years there has been a system to make sure girls are never in the majority, in spite of the fact that in terms of grades and test scores there were more qualified females than males.

And the higher up you go on the educational ladder, the worse it gets.

Women have trouble being admitted to graduate and professional training programs because of the ridiculous reasoning that "if a woman is not married, she will get married; if she is married, she will have children; if she has children, she cannot possibly be dedicated to a serious profession; if she has older children, she is too old to begin training." Men are not punished for getting married. Men are not punished because they become parents. Men are not told that having families means they aren't serious about their professions. Society doesn't limit men, but it punishes women simply for being women.

Many of the best scholarships are limited to men only.

There are very few colleges and universities that make it possible for a woman who has children to study. Not only are there few day-care centers, but very few institutions make part-time studies possible for women who want their degrees but must devote part of their time to domestic responsibilities. There are even universities where a woman must drop out if she is pregnant. (Men may return to college after they have finished military service; in many cases, women are not allowed to return after taking time off to have a baby.)

Even worse, however, is what can happen to you at college or university once you are there. It's like psychological warfare.

I have heard hard-working young friends of mine repeat awful things their professors have said to them.

"What's a cute girl like you worrying her head over political science for?" (I can't figure out the logic of that one. Did he mean that if you're cute you *are* stupid, or if you're cute you *should* be stupid. Or did he mean that if you're cute, you're supposed to be married and stop thinking altogether. Or did he mean only ugly people are interested in government and politics. At any rate, you can see the brilliance of his remark.)

"I know you do excellent work. I know your grades are marvelous. But are you really serious about what you are doing?" (What kind of question is that? Why does anybody work hard unless they're serious about what they're doing?)

"You're only going to get married, what do you want with a Master's?" (Never occurred to him that she could get married *and* be a biologist.)

"The mind of a woman is inferior to the mind of a man." (No comment on that one except to suggest that he's got the mind of a caveman, and you might answer with "ugh," if you ever hear the remark yourself.)

Aside from the put-downs about the quality of a woman's mind and the seriousness of her purposes, there are other even more serious problems.

One truly great difficulty is the quality of women's education. In many coed universities, women are shunted off into the usual "feminine" courses such as English, the arts, education and child care, nursing, library training. (I'll repeat, that while these are most honorable professions, women should have as full a spectrum of choices as men.)

In many women's colleges, the training isn't really practical. As you sit in the general courses that cover every imaginable liberal arts subject, it dawns on you slowly that you aren't being trained for anything. There are many educators who believe that a general liberal arts background is an excellent mind opener for everyone, men as well as women. The difference is that when men take liberal arts courses they are told they will eventually concentrate in one field, perhaps take a higher degree in their specialization. Or there will be training jobs open to them in business that are not open to women. If you ask questions about your unspecialized courses and your future in the job market, you may get the answer I once got.

"Job market? We're not preparing you here for the job market. We're preparing you to be the kind of well-educated, liberal-minded, well-rounded person who will make the sort of mother all children should have and the sort of wife who is most helpful to her husband."

(They were right. I had to take a secretarial course when I got out of college to get a job at all. And as for being a wife and mother, I learned how to do that on my own. It would have been much more helpful if I had been trained to *do* something while I was in college and also to have been offered special courses in the special problems women face. Too much to ask in four years of college? I don't think so.)

Often in so many colleges and universities women are given a sterile education that prepares them to do absolutely nothing in the real world.

Women in college are also too often given the kind of bad counseling they were given in high school. Instead of being encouraged to go into the field they happen to be good at (only 2 percent of the engineers in the United States are women, yet tests have shown that 40 percent of those with an aptitude for engineering are women), they are advised to enter fields that society considers feminine. (The trouble with feminine fields, let me remind you, is not that the work is not interesting or valuable but that they are low in both status and pay.) The counseling (not women's ability) is so bad, that only 6 percent of the women in college choose to specialize in economics, and only 5 percent of the college women receive professional degrees in fields like law, or architecture. Women are made to be afraid of these fields instead of being encouraged to fight sex discrimination. That women's minds are good enough to compete is proved by the fact that 68 percent of the women undergraduates have averages of B or better, compared to 54 percent of the men.

If part of the difficulty in getting the education you want and need is sex discrimination, the other part is what we have been discussing in the past few chapters—the bringing up of girls either to feel inferior or to act as if they were inferior in order to do the one thing that is expected of them, to get married.

Many studies have shown that college women are *afraid* of success, afraid that if they do too well they will not be considered feminine and men won't like them. Many do get good grades, but they do not always take their commitment to their work seriously.

Even those women whose parents have encouraged them to do well in school, to enter college to learn more, to develop themselves as human beings, often discover that what those same parents really had in mind was that college was the place to find a husband.

College women also have the usual problems with men. College women who are bright and who do well in class often feel that when they go out on dates, they have to play dumb so that men will like them. It isn't easy switching yourself around like that, so a lot of women just give up their own identities to play the traditional sex role. Too many women end up by being the doctor's wife instead of the doctor *and* a wife.

It's a sad moment for a woman who has worked hard to get into college, who has been rewarded for her academic achievement, when she trades in her mind, the possibility of an interesting career (or at least the ability to be financially independent), and her growth into a mature adult to be nothing but a wife. If she gives all she has achieved, she may end up being a girl forever, and never a woman.

Women at Work

It's a man's world out there.

Don't let anybody kid you that secretly women have power over men (they don't), that women really hold the purse strings of the nation (they don't), that women are happier serving and helping men (they aren't).

These are just some of the fairy tales everybody uses to keep women content with second place. There is an old saying that behind every successful man, there is a woman. Sure there is —about five steps behind, like a good Chinese wife.

Suppose now you've got your high school or college diploma. You've traded in your blue jeans for a pair of decent slacks or a skirt. You've understood that:

1) all people, male and female, married or not married, who want self-respect, self-reliance, and maturity instead of a childish dependency on others must develop their own skills, whatever they are, and use them

2) half the women in the United States work—32 million women work in the United States, constituting 40 percent of our labor force.

3) work and marriage go very nicely together—40 percent of all married women work (that old nonsense about the family unity and strength being threatened if a woman works is just that—nonsense!)

4) nine out of ten women work at some point during their lives.

5) even if women stay home to have babies, the average woman sends her last child off to school by the time she is thirty-five, which leaves about forty more years of her life to fill.

Furthermore, you've understood that useful, valued work is necessary to everyone's mental health, that your brain is just as good as a man's brain, that your ability to do a job is the same as a man's.

You've understood all of this. You're ready to face the working world and look for a job. Let's see what you're going to find.

Well, actually, what you're going to find is a mess.

You're going to find a lot of the same stupid business you've been hit over the head with all your life. Just as in the sandbox the boys got to do the trucking, and the digging, and the building while you got to bring the juice and cookies on your tea set; just as in high school and college, while the boys talked about things going on in the world, you got trapped into conversations about silver patterns, weddings, and clothes; in a business office, you'll find things haven't really progressed too far. Like all the people you've ever known—parents, teachers, friends, sweethearts, busdrivers, policemen—your employers will see you as a baby maker, a wife, and a mother, even if you're not. They will see you as a helper, rather than a doer. They will see you as all the things they wish you were, even if you are not: passive, weak, too emotional, unable to cope with important jobs, obedient, and definitely inferior to men. And because employers see you this way, they will give you the least desirable, lowest-paying jobs, with the least possibility for advancement. (We can beat the situation, though. Women all over the world are beginning to fight back.)

Right now, however, it's still pretty rough.

For one thing, the world has the peculiar idea that it doesn't have to pay women as much money as men for doing the same job. On the average, women earn sixty cents for every dollar that men earn. This is true for almost every kind of work from secretary to scientist—and the gap is getting bigger, not smaller. Women clerical workers earn less than three-fifths of what men clerical workers earn; women sales workers earn about two-fifths of what men earn in the same jobs; women managers and officials earn only a little more than half of what men earn in the same positions. Even if you're a doctor, a lawyer, or a scientist, you'll earn one-third less than the men. A woman with a college degree earns an average of about $6,700 per year; a male college graduate earns an average of about $11,800 per year.

The distribution of men and women in the salary scale is equally bad. One out of five of all women who work year round and full time earned less than $3,000 in 1968; two out of five earned only $3,000 to $5,000. Women were three times more likely than men to be in the under $5,000 earning bracket. In 1968, for clerical work, women earned an average of $4,800; men earned $7,350 for the same jobs. Women professional and technical workers got about $6,700 compared to about $10,000 for men. Saleswomen earned about $3,500; salesmen earned about $8,500. Women's roles at the top of the labor force continue to be very small indeed. Only 3 percent of those working year round and full time earned $10,000 or more in 1968. Three percent! As against 28 percent for men.

There is an Equal Pay Act. It was passed in 1963. And it was supposed to make it illegal to discriminate against women. In some cases, companies were forced to see that certain women got equal pay, even retroactively. But there are two problems with the Equal Pay Act. The government doesn't have enough staff to look into every situation. And the Equal Pay Act does not cover women in professional, executive, or administrative jobs.

Besides the unequal pay, women also suffer from being put into lesser-skilled jobs, where the pay is low and there isn't much hope of advancement either.

A publishing company I know advertises jobs for both men and women. When the men arrive for their interviews, they are given aptitude tests for managerial jobs. Women with the same college educations are given *typing* tests! The men will go up the ladder toward editorial and managerial positions; the women will remain, for the most part, in a dead end behind their typewriters. Even if some of the women make it into editorial positions, they will be paid less than the men. Airlines want college men for management; they want college women for stewardesses. Business offices want men for their on-the-job-training courses; they want women for secretaries and receptionists. (I know one secretary who knows more about running her boss's office than the boss himself. Why not? She's been doing it for fifteen years. Year after year she is asked to train new young junior managers to fill executive positions, while she continues to do the typing, answer the telephone, and bring the coffee. She knows enough to head the firm herself, but she will never be given the chance.) None of this is unusual. About one out of every five women with four years of college ends up in clerical, sales, service, or semiskilled factory jobs. Ninety-seven percent of all secretaries are women and only 2 percent of the nation's management personnel are women. And the situation is getting worse.

Women's roles in the better jobs have been going steadily down for a number of years. In 1940, we represented 45 percent of all workers in professional and technical positions; now, it's only 37 percent. It has taken 40 years for American women to advance from being 5 to 7 percent of our nation's doctors. They are only 8 percent of our scientists, 3 percent of our lawyers, only 2 percent of our engineers (this last number is odd, since, as we've mentioned, girls do very well in engineering aptitude tests in high school). In all these fields our women fare very badly compared to women in other industrialized countries of the world. In Russia, for example, women make up 75 percent of the total of physicians (although it should be said that the status of a physician in Russia is not as high as it is here). In France, 14 percent of all lawyers are women, in Denmark 50 percent of all law students are women.

We could go on with these numbers for hours, but they would only prove the same obvious point. The job scene for women, and to a strangely high degree in the United States, is unhealthy, unequal, and unfair.

Women work for the same reasons men do—for money, for the satisfaction of doing a good job, for fulfillment. Women therefore ought to have the same opportunities.

There are two main reasons women are not given the same chance as men. Men are prejudiced against women. And women are prejudiced against themselves. As children, they were all taught to think of females as inferior to males.

In a New York school, a poll was taken. The question was, "Would you vote for a woman to be president of the United States?" It wasn't too surprising that most of the boys flatly answered "no." What was surprising was that many of the girls answered the same way. Their answers included statements such as, "politics are for men," and "men have better minds for that sort of thing."

While it is perfectly true that men think badly of most women's abilities, it is also true that women have a bad image of themselves. In an office, if there is an opening for promotion, it will be given to a man, "because a man needs the money more." (Why? A woman can be the head of her own household or have a family that depends on her income.) Or "because one of these days she'll get married and quit." (Who says so? Many women don't quit their jobs just because they get married.) But the important point here is that not only do men treat us this way, but we accept it. We have been trained for so many years to take second place, that often we don't even fight back.

Too many women are successful in too many fields for men to be able to say any longer that women don't have the brains to do a job well. There are famous women who are in politics, who are on the New York Stock Exchange, who run advertising agencies, who are leading physicists, anthropologists, corporation directors, writers, retailers, publishers, sales managers, doctors, and lawyers. What men have taken to saying now is, "maybe she has the brains, but she isn't emotionally stable enough," or "women are difficult to deal with," or "any woman who's *that* successful has to be a little nutty, (or too aggressive, or impossible to understand, and so forth)."

It isn't easy working in what is so far still a man's world. You'll either get the worst jobs, or if you get a good one, you'll have to fight twice as hard as a man to keep it. If you are a black woman, you can double the difficulty. (Almost 50 percent of all minority women workers are in service work, and half of these are maids earning only $1,500 a year.)

You'll be watched more closely, and you'll get a lot more criticism.

You'll be left out of important business meetings and barred from business clubs and then told you don't know what's going on.

You'll be insulted and belittled if you don't act "feminine" and then held back from promotion if you do act "feminine."

If you have children, people will worry that you're going to quit your job. If you don't have children, they'll call you unnatural.

Because many women still say they are working "only until I get married," "just to help out for a while," "just to put my husband through school," women's image in the working world is less bright than it should be. The fact is that statistics show that women hold their jobs longer than men do, now. (So don't let some male boss tell you women's job-turnover rate is higher—it isn't.) Also, women take off less time for illness than men, including time taken off to have babies.

You'll be told you're more emotional than men. Nonsense. It's just that in our society, women are allowed to show their emotions and men are not supposed to show theirs.

It is generally accepted that males are more aggressive than females, and that females are more perceptive than males (this is not true of all males or all females, only on the average). Remember, it takes both aggression and perception to do the work of the world. Understanding a situation is just as necessary as getting in there and fighting about it.

In most countries of the world, all the important decisions about life are made by men. And the world is a mess. It may be that the talents of both sexes are necessary if we're going to improve things. Certainly we shouldn't complain about the state of the world unless we're willing to shoulder half the responsibility, or maybe unless we're willing to fight to get half the responsibility.

It's true that the working world is difficult for women. Life in general is difficult for people who are sat on. The thing to do is stand up. That way, you remove the lap, and there is no place for anybody to sit. It also leaves the legs free for walking or running wherever you want to go.

Women and the Arts

In discussions with men on the subject of women's liberation, there are two things I keep hearing over and over from those who are "male chauvinist pigs." (A "male chauvinist pig" is a man who thinks, or behaves as if he thinks, that women are not as good as men. Or he may think of us as equal in importance, but only as long as we keep to women's work—that is, taking care of *him, his* house, *his* babies, and *his* interests. He will call this separate-but-equal. Only somehow separate-but-equal never ends up being equal to the ones who are separate.)

What men say most often is, "Laws have been passed giving you job equality. So if you are as good as men are, how come you haven't gotten better pay and better jobs?"

The answer to that one is easy. You know it already. It's called *discrimination*. Once this is explained to them, the MCP's (male chauvinist pigs) seem to accept it as truth. But then their eyes light up with that triumphant superiority we all know so well and dare us to answer the next question.

"If, as you claim, women's brains are just as good as men's brains, how come there is no female Michelangelo? How come there is no female Shakespeare?"

Why is there no female Michelangelo? Why are there no women's names on the lists of greatness in the visual arts? It is a question that makes men feel terribly smug and makes women feel just plain terrible. It is a question that, if you aren't careful, seems to supply its own answer: "because women just don't have it in them to be great artists."

(Don't panic. It isn't the right answer, because it isn't the right question.)

Generally, when men attack with the question, "Why are there no great women artists?" a feminist who is proud of being a woman will scramble around in her mind to come up with a list of well-known woman painters and sculptors—Berthe Morisot, Angelica Kauffmann, Rosa Bonheur, Artemisia Gentileschi, Marie Ann Elisabeth Vigée-Lebrun, Käthe Kollwitz, Louise Nevelson, Mary Cassatt. A proud feminist will try to prove, by using the names of these women, that there is a history of greatness in the art of women, that it has simply been neglected, overlooked. Champions of women's equality also fall into the trap of trying to puff up the achievements of a limited number of women artists. The trouble is, it doesn't work. The sad truth is, that no matter how hard we search, we can't come up with many female artists or any as great as Michelangelo or Rembrandt or Picasso. There just haven't been any.

And it doesn't help to think about what might have been. For instance when one looks at the magnificent needlework of the past, often done by nuns, it makes one feel as if real talent was trapped into a sideline. It isn't a matter of "why are there no great women artists." It's a matter of "why haven't women been *allowed* to be great artists!"

Once again, women never stood a chance. Only part of great art is genius. The other two parts are study and encouragement. Think of the stories of great male artists. The young Giotto, a lowly shepherd boy, was discovered drawing pictures of his sheep on a stone by an older, great artist named Cimabue who was so impressed by the drawings that he immediately invited the boy to be his pupil.

If young Giotto had been a girl, she would have been told to learn to cook instead. In those days, only males were invited to study under the great masters, never females. Only males were allowed to join the Art Guilds, never females. Art is only partly instinct and talent. It also takes a tremendous amount of training. Girls might dabble on their own; they were never allowed training. Michelangelo, it is said, did more drawing than studying his lessons as a child. For his efforts, he got to study under the master Ghirlandaio, who taught and encouraged him and said of him finally, "This boy knows more than I do."

If Michelangelo had been a girl, her mother might have said, "You draw nicely, dear. Now wash the shirts, give the baby his dinner, and sweep the kitchen for me, there's a good girl." She would have been given little time to draw, less encouragement, and no training at all.

To be an artist requires, above all, hours to oneself to practice one's profession. Until recently, and even now, women have had to struggle for time. Females were simply never allowed two minutes off from their household duties to accomplish very much of anything. No artist, male or female, ever made it on artistic genius alone. Time to practice; places to study like art academies or master's studios; encouragement by society, one's fellow artists, one's parents—these are all part of what makes greatness out of talent. What is surprising is not that there are no really great women artists, but that there are any at all.

By the nineteenth century, a few heroic women managed to get themselves taught and to emerge as painters. All were either daughters of artists or were close to artists who helped them. It took a tremendous amount of courage and rebellion against society (which approved of women only if they were wives and mothers) to choose a career at all, much less a career in the arts, which had for thousands of years been reserved for men only.

In the twentieth century, it is easier to get oneself taught. But it is almost as difficult as ever to find encouragement and serious acceptance if you are a woman. (I have a woman friend who is an artist. She says that when she talks with men artists, they still seem to think that women's only place in art is as an object to paint, or as an inspiration to the artist. My friend says it's time we stopped modeling for pictures instead of painting them, time we stopped inspiring others and started inspiring ourselves.) But unlike men, we still have to struggle with the guilt society makes us feel for choosing to have a career, for not devoting ourselves entirely to being wives and mothers.

While the question about great women composers (there were none in the past—although there are a few doing excellent work now) must be answered in about the same way as the question about great women artists, the history of great women writers is a little different. There is no Wilma Shakespeare, it is true. Women, four hundred years ago, were not even educated, much less let out of the house to traipse off to London to learn the theater business. If Wilma had managed to learn to read on her own and was found mooning over books, her mother would have told her to mind the stew and then married her off like a shot. If by some chance Wilma had managed to find her way to London's theaters and asked for a job, the managers would have laughed in her face. No women were allowed even to act (men played the women's roles) much less get enough theater training to write a play.

But if we have produced no playwrights, we have produced great novelists. Jane Austen, George Eliot, Emily and Charlotte Brontë, and George Sand of the nineteenth century Western world, Lady Murasaki of tenth-century Japan (note that a woman produced the first great novel ever written), to name a few, have written novels equal in artistic greatness to those written by the great male novelists, Dickens, Thackeray, Tolstoy. Women were barred from politics and war, so it is not surprising that no nineteenth-century woman wrote a novel like Tolstoy's *War and Peace*. But on all other aspects of nineteenth-century society (except for sex which neither men nor women were allowed to discuss publicly) there is a wealth of witty, profound, and passionate literature written by women. In the twentieth century, women have produced brilliant work, too. Think of Willa Cather, Katherine Anne Porter, Dorothy Parker, Virginia Woolf, Susan Sontag, Eudora Welty, Carson McCullers. Many people will argue and say that the literature written so far by women is not as great as that written by men. Certainly it is true we have had fewer great writers.

Again it must be said that women have had a hard battle for acceptance. The critics were so prejudiced against writers who were women that in the eighteenth century, women published anonymously, and in the nineteenth century, many used masculine names. Charlotte and Emily Brontë used the names Currer and Ellis Bell; George Eliot's name was really Mary Ann Evans; George Sand's name was Amandine Dudevant. And not only did critics belittle novels if they were known to be written by women, but all of society treated any woman who worked at a profession as if she were a freak. Creativity in women was supposed to be confined to the bearing and raising of children, the arranging of flowers, the giving of dinner parties, and many people considered it immoral as well as unladylike for women to take time away from their housework and children to pursue other work.

By the middle of the last century, it finally became respectable for a woman to have literary ambitions—to want to publish and make money from writing—but many critics went on sneering. Even today, there are critics who call women writers "lady novelists" and whose general attitude seems to be "it's a wonder they write at all, much less write well."

But at least, unlike the other arts, the writing of poetry, essays, and novels was possible for women. It was something that could be done at home and alone. No need, like a painter, to go out in search of an academy, an art school, a model to paint; or like a composer, to have to have musical training. Women at home, even if they were not formally educated at schools like their brothers, could read books for themselves and learn how to write by reading. And then, writing could be dropped at a moment's notice to meet the demands of family life. It might also be added that writing materials are cheap— no need for costly art supplies or instruments.

It still isn't easy for women to achieve the discipline and dedication it takes to be a professional in the creative arts. Gifts, brains, and genius are the property of both sexes; but for these to develop there must be encouragement, acceptance, education, and above all, hours and hours of free time. The emancipation of women is spectacularly new. We have begun to develop as writers, as artists, as composers. But emancipation does not result in instant achievement. Geniuses are not born every hour. Even among men, who have had so much more opportunity to develop, the really great are few in number.

How many times have you heard, "Women don't need to be creative. Making babies is the greatest act of creation there is." Making babies is indeed wonderful, and certainly there wouldn't be any life anywhere without that particular form of activity. But making babies is nature's miracle, not the miracle of a single creative mind. And did you ever hear anybody tell a man that fathering a baby was all he had to do to be creative?

We must beware of saying to ourselves: babies are enough to create, babies are like beautiful pictures, poems, symphonies. Babies are great. But they aren't like pictures, poems, or songs, they are like babies. In the history of mankind and womankind (peoplekind?), half the geniuses ever born, the half that were women, have died without having been allowed to follow their stars. The future must be different. We can't afford to waste human talent on that scale.

Women's Image in Advertising and What They Do to You in Department Stores

Of all the woman-haters that have ever lived, advertisers rank among the worst. Every time you turn on the television set, the commercials are there to tell you every few minutes, day after day, year after year, that you are an idiot, and a ridiculous idiot at that. You can be seen looking gorgeous and sexy, twitching every female muscle to catch a boy or the attention of a husband; you can be seen on your knees waxing a floor, bending over a stove, cleaning, washing, diapering a baby. And not only do you spend your entire day doing the dull, routine work of being a servant to your family, but you are *thrilled* to be doing it!

If you are ever seen outside the kitchen (much less outside

the home), you will be found serving men in offices (as secretaries) or airplanes (as stewardesses) instead of in the house. Not that it matters to your television self what you are doing, since your only interest in life anyway is what the advertisers call the "male reward." Advertisers snigger over what they feel is a sure bet: that you'll do any kind of work, go through any kind of drudgery, spend any amount of time, money, and agony on girdles, clothes, and makeup, crawl, cringe, and scrape—anything, so long as at the end of it, some male pats you on the head like a good girl (dog?).

Advertising puts woman in her place as household servant and sex object and keeps her there. Advertising is a terrible propaganda machine for a male supremacist society; it tells both men and women that women are stupid childlike creatures whose only abilities are those of sex partner, housekeeper, baby maker, and servant. And the commercials run so often, and they are seen by so many millions of people that, like the Chinese water torture, the drops of poison go on dripping until everybody is convinced that there must be some truth to the commercial images. On and on goes the same image: men run the world; and women are only fit to amuse and serve the men. It is humiliating, degrading, and disgusting. Worst of all, the image is a lie. Nearly half the women in this country work, but you'd never know that from looking at American advertising. (Sadly, they also do 98 percent of the housework—but they don't love it, it exhausts them.)

Sexist advertising begins at a very early age to show girls how silly and unimportant they are. Think of the toys that are advertised on television. The boys are shown creating things with blocks or learning with science kits. But for the girls there are Barbie dolls so they can learn young what they are supposed to do when they grow up: be adorable and catch a man! What this kind of thing produces is a whole generation of girls who will grow up to be thirty-year-old Barbie dolls. Another advertisement just as hateful is Johnson & Johnson's

Creme Rinse for Children. Children? Have you ever seen a
boy in that commercial? Never. While boys jump through mud
puddles (so their mothers can wash their clothes three times a
day with Frab or Toad or whatever-kind-of-soap it is), a little
blond girl with or without her little brunette friend lisps out
how shiny her hair is. It's enough to make you want to slap, not
her, but the sponsor.

When the commercial-advertisement girl gets too old for
dolls, her only interest in life becomes boys—not herself or the
world or the work she will do. According to television, a girl's
only activity is to get a boy, any boy, quick.

If you take the advice of television commercials, you will
grin insanely at him with ultra brite toothpaste on your teeth;
you will chew Dentyne or suck a Cert in his face so he'll kiss
you; you will use Colgate, the "mouthwash for lovers," or pre-
sumably you won't have one; you will drink Tab until you're
so skinny he won't be able to see you if you turn sideways; you
will Clairol your hair blond, soak in Sardo bath oil, and switch
to Scope mouthwash if the Colgate hasn't floored him yet.
(While you're doing all this, you'd better cross your fingers
that he hasn't gone off with some girl who's got more interesting things on her mind.)

Not that the television people really think any of you has a
mind. How about the ad from Parker Pens? "You might as
well give her a gorgeous pen to keep her checkbook unbal-
anced with. A sleek and shining pen will make her feel prettier.
Which is more important to any girl than solving mathematical
mysteries."

And then when you've finally done the one thing everybody
wanted you to do and gotten married, are you at long last
given the respect due to any human being? Don't be funny.
Now you have really become an absurd joke to the advertisers.

According to them, the only thing you truly get ecstatic
about, the only thing that really turns you on, is housework.
There is a Fab commercial in which a whole row of women

out in their backyards are singing with hysterical joy among
the flapping sheets while waving boxes of their favorite deter-
gent. (Can you imagine what their husbands would do if they
came home and found their wives dancing and shrieking over
their wash—pack them all off on a freighter probably.)

And how about the love affairs women are supposed to be
having with their suds and cleansers and household products?
There's a man called Wally who comes out of the wall, flexes
his muscles, and shows the dazzled housewife just how clean
her wall can be with Big Wally's help. There's the Man from
Glad who practically saves her life. And let's not forget the
romantic White Knight, or the half-naked Mr. Clean (what is
he supposed to be, the thrill of the day while hubby is at the
office?), or the mysterious Janitor-in-a-Drum. Really! Just how
crazy do the advertisers think women are?

One of the more truly idiotic commercials concerns a housewife who hears that her child's teacher is coming over. Does
she worry about her child? Not on your life! She cleans the
whole living room and practically swoons over how shiny
Lemon Pledge gets her table.

You'd think, watching commercials, that women spent their
entire lives, not just in their houses, but in their kitchens.
Youthful housewives are constantly pictured surrounded by
washing machines, dryers, ovens, blenders, coffee pots, toasters,
standing on newly tiled, freshly waxed floors. And they talk
about nothing but children, the wash, cooking, and cleaning.
It's a joke. But it's a sad joke, because while it's all made to
seem beautiful and glamorous and meaningful, the reality is
that the world thinks so little of housework and gives it so little
status, that domestic work is about the lowest-paying job you
can get.

Yet the ads try to fool you into thinking housework can be
satisfying enough to fill your whole life. They do this by telling
you how happy you'll be if you can see your face in a shiny
clean plate or a shiny clean floor. The truth is that there is

simply nothing very challenging about everyday cleaning, no matter how hard the ad people try to convince us there is. Part of the reason they work so hard is the fact that surveys have shown that many women are *afraid* to admit they don't like housework; advertisers are playing on that psychological fear very cruelly.

Another way they try to sell their products is by making women feel guilty if they aren't doing their housework in the proper way. This is especially true of the advertisements for cooking products. The admen don't really believe the world will end if the kitchen floor isn't spotless and forever waxed or that families all over the country will gag unless their chicken is fried in Crisco—but they try to make women believe it. They try to make women believe that to neglect such sacred duties will bring them dishonor in the eyes of the world and the loss of their families' love.

The main thing these ads and commercials accomplish is to make women feel their chief role in life is to please men, serve their families, and stay in the kitchen as much as possible. They also reinforce men's concepts of "a woman's place is in the home." But worst of all they picture us as idiots, or at best as a race of not-very-bright children. Since 55 percent of the women in the United States are high-school graduates and 25 percent have attended college, it is both an insult and an outrage that we are still being shown to the world as mental retardates.

Even the commercials geared to men are demeaning put-downs for women. There is a Winchester cigar commercial in which a woman is shown with a man whom she drops cold to follow another man just because he smokes a Winchester cigar. In automobile ads there are pretty girls who seem about to be given away with the cars. And then there are the male-type ads that leave women out altogether. You never see women business executives, women doctors, women motorcyclists. It's always men, never women, who are in control, who are active, who do the thinking, while women are given away like coupons, or stand around admiringly, or are simply left out altogether. (You know, of course, where you can find them—in the next commercial, overjoyed to find that Dash gets their clothes clean in the new bigger-and-better washing machine.)

Speaking of bigger-and-better goodies, there is another way society takes advantage of lonely and frustrated housewives. Women's magazines, television, and department stores are all trying to con women into thinking they will find fulfillment in buying more "things"—especially if those "things" are either for home-and-family or to make her look more fascinating to her husband (clothes, cosmetics). If a woman can be brainwashed (and after so much hammering on the head, many women can't help but be) into feeling that her whole life can be changed by a new washing machine, a new shower curtain, or a new pair of false eyelashes, department store sales go up and up and up.

Department stores play with your mind in another way, too. Since many women live lonely lives within the walls of their houses and fear that life is passing them by, department stores offer women an experience, a lesson, in what's going on in the world of new products, new discoveries, new fashions. They make women feel more in touch with the outside world. They also make a woman feel she is an expert in *something,* even if it's only the right polish to use, the newest thing in drapery material, or the best of all possible suds.

Bargain sales are another way stores cheat women. They have managed to make a woman feel virtuous, like a good little housewife, if she buys something on sale. A sale price makes her think, "I'm doing a good job as a housewife. I'm contributing to the welfare of my family in the same way my husband does when he brings home a paycheck." The sad part is, she will buy anything, even if she doesn't need it, just to have that virtuous feeling.

But remember, the commercials are only mirrors. It is society that creates the narrow roles in the first place. And maybe these mirrors can teach us a lesson. If, as girls and women, we look long enough and hard enough at those humiliating mirrors, it might make a lot of us realize how sad our condition is if our only goals in life are cleaner kitchen floors and diapers, or a new mascara and blonder hair.

That stuff is all right in its place, but it's not enough. And if you doubt it, just switch the image to a man. Would it be enough for a man to have the cleanest floors in the neighborhood? To have the prettiest complexion?

Well, if it isn't enough for him, then it isn't enough for you!

There's Something Wrong with Your Rights

Did you know that nowhere in the Constitution of the United States does it state that women are citizens? Women have never been legally declared persons in this country, not by the Founding Fathers (there were, naturally, no Founding Mothers), not by the Constitution, not by the Supreme Court. The Fifteenth Amendment guarantees the right to vote to all U.S. citizens, whatever their color or race and whether they had been born free or born slaves, but this did *not* include women.

Women fought for the abolition of slavery. When the battle was won, black men got the vote. Black women did not. Nor white women either.

To win the vote, women ran 56 referendum campaigns; 804

campaigns in the states; 19 campaigns in 19 consecutive Congresses. The effort to win our right to vote took 52 years, until in 1920, the Nineteenth Amendment was passed.

Those regions of the country that were most racist were also the most antifeminist. Of the ten states that refused to agree to the Nineteenth Amendment, nine were southern. The tenth was Delaware. The white male looked down on blacks and women alike. Even Thomas Jefferson said that women, slaves, and babies should be kept away from political decisions. The region where women fared best was the West, where they had fought and pioneered alongside their men. Wyoming refused to become a state and join the Union unless its women, who had already been given voting rights within the territory, could keep those rights. "We will remain out of the Union a hundred years rather than come in without the women," they said.

But even though we finally got the right to vote, women still have very little actual political power. This is partly due to male discrimination against women, to their feeling that women are not intellectually capable of making important political decisions or that women are too emotionally unstable to be trusted with the affairs of the nation. It is also partly due to the fact that many women, themselves, believe this to be true and would not run for office or vote for women.

Only a handful of women have been elected to the Senate and Congress of the United States. In 1972, women held only 13 out of 535 seats in Congress. There were only a token number of women federal judges, and there had never been a woman on the Supreme Court. There have been a few women governors, but these were largely elected not for themselves, but as stand-ins for their husbands who were not allowed to run again under state law.

In some countries, women are much worse off. Swiss women are not even allowed to vote on a federal level. And in Arab countries like Saudi Arabia and Iraq, women have no political rights at all.

In the Communist countries, the story is about the same as it is here. Out of 1,378 seats in the Soviet Council of Union and the Council of Nationalities only 25 were held by women in 1972. In China there were only 290 women among the 4,060 people who held national legislative office. (China has taken great pride in freeing its women from household bondage and providing day-care centers for children so the women are free to pursue their work. So far, so good. But it's still the men who run the government.)

In the whole world, there are only three women heads of state who have held any real power: Golda Meir was chosen premier of Israel in 1969; Indira Gandhi was made prime minister of India in 1966; and Sirimavo Bandaranaike of Ceylon was premier from 1960 to 1965.

Without power, we cannot help make or change the laws. ("Make policy, not coffee" is the motto of the Women's Political Caucus.) We may lobby, campaign, and fight, but we must run for office if we truly want to be in a position to make changes in the laws that are unfair to women.

And there are many unfair laws.

There was once a debate in the legislature of Tennessee. It was stated at the time that women had no souls—therefore, the law would not permit them to own property.

Many of our problems with the laws in this country began when we were not declared citizens, continued when we were refused the vote, and are still aggravated because we do not have very much political power. Among the worst of these problems are the laws for married women about MONEY.

Although 40 percent of the married women in this country work outside the home, 60 percent are housewives. A housewife means you work up to fourteen hours a day as nursemaid, dietitian, food buyer, chauffeur, dishwasher, housekeeper, laundress, seamstress, practical nurse, maintenance person, gardener, and cook—for nothing. No salary, no insurance, no Social Security, no pension plan. Food, clothing, and shelter are generally provided. Anything else you get depends on the good nature of your husband. And you have to *ask* for it. You have no *right* to it.

In all but eight states, a husband's earnings are his separate, personal property. His wife has no legal claim on his money or on any property in his name. Even in the eight states where there is a thing called community property laws and everything is supposedly owned by both husband and wife, the property is still under the husband's sole control. In four states, even a wife's *own* earnings are under the complete control of her husband. In some other states, a married woman does not have the freedom to start a business without her husband's permission.

What all this means is that housewives can work their whole lives long and never have the lawful right to one red cent!

A woman I know not only did the household chores for her family and brought up the children, but on top of that helped her husband by working in his florist shop many hours every day. After twenty years, she wanted to leave him. But after all those years of work, both inside and outside the home, she still had no right to any money. She cannot claim back salary because she was working for her husband; she cannot claim a share of the business, because that, of course, belongs to him solely since it is in his name. She is out of luck altogether.

When there is a divorce, people are always talking about how unfair it is to the man to have to pay alimony. There is always the picture of men working hard, and divorced women just sitting around eating boxes of chocolates. The facts are quite different. Although by law, the husband must pay for child support, many women either don't get alimony, or get such a low amount they can barely manage. And this, after the wife has worked for the husband for nothing as a housekeeper for all the years they were married. Most women think of alimony, not as a charity gift, but as back pay for the work they did. According to economists at the Chase Manhattan Bank, housewives are doing free work worth at least $257.53 a week on the current labor market.

When people make fun of a housewife's work, it is only because it is a *woman* who is doing it. Men who cook are chefs; women who cook are just cooks. Men who handle finances are accountants; women are just bookkeepers. The Labor Department's *Dictionary of Occupational Titles,* which grades 22,000 occupations on a skill scale from a high of 1 to a low of 887, rates homemakers near the bottom at 878 (along with foster mothers, nursery school teachers, and practical nurses).

Even women downgrade themselves by saying, "I don't work. I'm just a housewife." Now there are lots of people, men as well as women, who are happier working at home than working in the outside world. This is true of many artists of both sexes and of people who like to cook. Staying at home should be allowed to men as well as to women. And what's wrong with a woman working at an outside job to support her husband, if he's the one who prefers the housekeeping?

But when it is the woman who stays home, and since she is the one whose rights to money is the problem, the laws must be changed so that she is paid in some way, legally, for her work. Getting love for what you do is wonderful, but if there's trouble, you can't live on love. Either, 1) housewives should be paid a salary by their husbands (or some part of his income should be hers by law); 2) there should be a law to make sure that if the marriage ends, she is paid back salary; or 3) housework should be placed in the category of jobs covered by the Social Security system, so that she can collect money as other workers do after retirement.

The point of all this is to let a woman choose her career. She should be able to take a job outside the home or work within the home; either way, she should be paid, legally, for the work she does.

And why are there no laws for business deductions for married women who work? A man can take a business lunch off his taxes, but a woman cannot take the price of a baby-sitter off her taxes.

In every state, a wife's residence is said, legally, to be where her husband lives. If he moves and she doesn't want to move with him, he can sue her for desertion.

Juvenile delinquency laws are unfair to girls in many states. Until recently, under New York's Family Court Act, a boy who ran away from home (without just cause) after the age of sixteen would not have been returned to his home. A girl would have been returned to her home until she was eighteen.

There were two teenagers in Westchester, New York; a boy, seventeen, and a girl, seventeen. The parents of both teenagers brought them to court because both stayed out too late at night, both hung around with undesirable companions, and both had contracted a venereal disease. The girl, because she was under eighteen, was declared by the court to be a "Person in Need of Supervision," and was sent to a state training school for rehabilitation. The boy was let go. "Boys will be boys," said the judge. Since he was over sixteen, and as long as he had not committed a crime, no action was taken against him, as was the case with the girl.

A girl may receive a longer sentence in some states than a boy for the same action. If, in New York, a fifteen-year-old boy and a fifteen-year-old girl ran away, the boy would be held in training school only until he was eighteen. The girl would be held until she was twenty.

There are some acts that are crimes only if they are done by women. A girl may be put in reform school for up to four years if she has had sexual experiences with several boys. The court may convict her of "promiscuity." Naturally, if a boy has sexual experiences with several girls—well, "boys will be boys" again, and there is no penalty. (In July 1972, the Court of Appeals of New York State finally decided there was no justification for the age-sex distinction. The Court has now rejected such outdated notions. In New York now, girls are not censured more than boys for sexual misconduct. In many states, however, the sex distinction is still part of the law.)

Two other areas of discrimination against women are housing and credit. In many places, single women find it difficult to rent a house or an apartment, even if they have perfectly good jobs and can well afford the rent. The grounds for the landlord's discrimination is that women, like children, can't be trusted to pay their bills. Women who are divorced have special troubles. In New York City, a recently divorced woman with a young child had difficulty getting an apartment because landlords kept insisting "that all divorced women give noisy parties and never pay their rent on time." What made this particular story doubly idiotic was that a quieter, more sedate woman never lived!

In some areas of the United States a single woman may have trouble getting credit to make large purchases. She will have to get a male relative to co-sign if she wants to buy a home or if she wants a credit card or a charge account. I know of one woman who had been the sole support of her family for ten years. Her husband had been seriously ill and hadn't been able to work. But despite this, when the time came to buy a house, the papers had to be signed by him!

Thousands of women all over the country have organized to fight for the rights of women under the law. Women have accomplished a great deal, but there is more fighting to do.

The Equal Rights Amendment was passed by Congress in March 1972. This amendment would forbid discrimination based on sex by any law or action of federal, state, or local government. But the amendment still has to be ratified by 38 states, and there is much lobbying to be done in order to make sure the Equal Rights Amendment goes through.

The powers of the Equal Employment Opportunity Commission to enforce nondiscrimination in employment must be strengthened. The Equal Pay Act must be strengthened and enforced, so that professional, administrative, and executive women will get the same pay as men for the same work.

New rules of the Equal Employment Opportunity Commission will give more rights to pregnant women employees. The new rules say that to deny a woman a job because she is pregnant is a violation of the Civil Rights Act of 1964. They also say that pregnancy must be regarded as an illness and therefore women who take maternity leave must be given sick pay.

Women are also fighting for the right to their own bodies, the right to make their own decisions about whether they want to bear children or not. All over the world, women are refusing to have unwanted children—30 million abortions are performed each year. But until recently they've had to duck male-made laws against abortions, and often had to go to quacks. In some states, you could only get an abortion if the doctors agree that having a baby would injure your health. In some states and in England, abortion was legal if the psychiatrists agreed your mental health would be endangered. In Italy and Mexico, abortions are illegal, but they are cheap and easy to get. In Bulgaria, Hungary, Japan, Poland, Czechoslovakia, and Yugoslavia, abortion is legal. In Scandinavia, women need psychiatric and hospital approval. Conditions differ everywhere, but in very few places have women had the right to decide for themselves whether they want or do not want to remain pregnant. Feminists feel that just as women who are against abortion should have a right to their opinion, women who believe in abortion should have a right to have one if they want.

Another very important fight is for day-care centers, so that mothers who want to work have clean, well-staffed places to leave their children during working hours. These day-care centers should either be free or be inexpensive enough so that working people can afford them easily.

The time has come (actually, it came a long time ago, but

women don't seem to have talked to each other about their common problems until recently) when politics and lawmaking can no longer be left solely in the hands of men. We must protect ourselves—housewives, workers, teenage girls—with equal laws, equal pay for equal work, equal job opportunities; we must fight for day-care centers and the right to control our own bodies; we must have a voice in the affairs of the nation, whether the affairs are "women's issues" or poverty or racism or war. It isn't easy to break the male prejudice barrier. As Shirley Chisholm, New York Congresswoman and 1972 candidate for the presidency of the United States, once said, "As a black person, I am no stranger to race prejudice. But the truth is that in the political world I have been far oftener discriminated against because I am a woman than because I am black."

But we've got to fight—fight and shout and scream and holler, if that's what it takes. And if that ruins our image as sweet little ladylike darlings—well, where did being sweet little ladylike darlings get us anyway, except into a television commercial behind a dishpan!

The Beautiful Imbecile

Do you look like Elizabeth Taylor, Marilyn Monroe, Brigitte Bardot, Raquel Welch, or Miss Teenage America? Do you have long legs, long eyelashes, a small waist, a big bust, narrow hips, large eyes, shining hair, a perfect smile, and a fetching walk?

No? Shoot yourself.

You might as well get it over with now as spend the rest of your life in the agony most women go through with their looks, the agony of the beauty game. It's a game you're forced to play from the moment you are born until the day you die, and if for a little while you forget to play, there is always somebody around to remind you. A girl, your boyfriend, your mother, a salesman in a commercial—somebody is always there to suggest you weigh too much or too little, you're too tall or too short, you need an uplift bra or a padded bra or no bra, you need a cream rinse or a wig, a new eyeliner, face cream, or lipstick, a shorter skirt or newer pants. Whatever it is, you need something, because you're certainly not all right the way you are.

It's a terrible game, because there's no way you can win. For one thing, the rules keep changing, so even if you look all right now, wait ten minutes and you'll be out of style again. And then, even if you happen to be the rarest of beauties, one day the wrinkles and the gray hair will come, to depress you for the rest of your life.

It's infuriating, the way we've been made miserable over our looks, the way we've been pushed into such a frantic pursuit of beauty.

Of course, it's hardly surprising. Even before a baby is born, parents sit around crossing their fingers and hoping that if it's a girl she'll be pretty. When she's born, they inspect closely. If she's pretty, there's a general sigh of relief. But even if she's a dud in the looks department, they'll say, "Maybe she'll be pretty when she grows up," or "at least she'll have a pretty figure," or "well, she'll always be pretty to us."

Pretty, pretty, pretty. Does it matter if she has talent or brains? Not on your life!

And as a little girl grows up, what does she see around her? She sees her mother trying to be pretty for her father even while she's scrubbing the floor. She sees ads in magazines, commercials on television, all telling her that a girl had better be pretty or she'll never get a man. In movies, it's always the pretty girl who is loved. Wherever she looks, there are beautiful female models, in her father's *Playboy* magazine, on the covers of books, on the huge billboards on the highways, in the paintings in museums. It can't help but make her think that if a woman isn't pretty, she's hardly a woman at all.

As she grows up, people are always harping on her appearance. Don't get your pretty dress dirty. Can't you wear something prettier than those jeans? Why don't you comb your hair so you'll look prettier? Is it any wonder that by the time a girl is in her teens, she holds the secret belief that it is more important to be pretty than to be anything else in the world? Society has made such a big deal about beauty that most girls, given the choice, would pick beauty instead of brains, would rather look like Miss Universe than win the Nobel Prize for physics as Maria Goeppert Mayer did in 1963. Or be among the three or four greatest novelists of the nineteenth century as George Eliot was.

An interesting point should be made about George Eliot. As great as she was, she agonized all her life over not being pretty. So did Charlotte Brontë. Great male writers like Dante and Emerson were ugly, too, but nobody ever bothered them about it. Critics harp on whether great women are pretty because they would rather think of them as women than as great minds. When you see a story in a newspaper about an important woman executive or read that a woman has gained a political position, how often have you read "And she is pretty, too"? Do they ever comment on how handsome a male judge is or on the hairdo of a male executive? Just once I'd like to read, "George Smithers, hair curled enchantingly over his ears, dressed in a divine double-breasted, pinstriped, London-tailored suit, has just been elected Governor of. . . ."

What women have gone through to be beautiful has often been painful and is almost always uncomfortable. For centuries the women of China bound their feet because the ideal foot was tiny. Binding the feet tightly made bones break, toes drop off, and often gangrene set in, bringing death. A thousand years ago in Japan, women who wanted to be fashionable had to paint their teeth black and wear their hair so long they could hardly stand up under the weight of it, much less get around the palace. In primitive societies where it is fashionable to be fat, women force-feed themselves like geese. In many societies, including ours today, girls have gone through the pain of piercing their ears. Women undergo surgery to have their faces lifted, their skin peeled, their breasts filled with silicone, their noses and thighs reshaped. They starve and wear tight girdles to be thinner, they endure the pain of electrolysis to rid their bodies of hair.

Simply, what women do to be pretty is go through hell. And even if *you* decide not to torture yourself about the way you look, the rest of the world will remind you daily whether you are attractive or not.

The reason for the beauty game is that girls are rarely brought up to be fully developed human beings. We are not brought up to be work companions or mental companions for men, but primarily sexual companions. Like animals, we are supposed to use our bodies, but not our minds. We are told from the beginning that men like their women beautiful, not bright. When Martin Luther spoke of women, he said, "No dress or garment is less becoming to a woman than a show of intelligence." And girls today are still being told never to let a man find out how smart they are—unless, of course, they are so gorgeous no one will listen to them anyhow, on the theory that if you're all *that* beautiful, you can't possibly have a brain in your head.

Unfortunately, women have been brought up to feel the same way men feel. Just as men expect women to be beautiful, women expect it of themselves. If a woman is intelligent, if she goes ahead, in spite of everybody's disapproval, and gets herself a college education, a degree, an interesting or intellectual job, she very often worries whether she has become unsexy because of it. That's why so many women doctors, professors, executives, writers will wear a frilly blouse or have their hair teased or show their legs under a short skirt—to reassure themselves and the people they meet that even though they're smart, they're still sexy.

The miniskirt and the teeny-weeny bikini deserve mention here. Girls hear older people say that young women today are more sexually liberated than ever before, and if you don't believe it, look at the clothes. This just isn't true. The revealing clothes don't express *our* sexuality, they express our desire to please men as we were brought up to do. In the Victorian age, men preferred their women to look innocent, so women wore skirts down to the floor and buttons up to their chins. Then men got bored with the innocent look, and they now want us to look sexy.

But you're still only supposed to look that way, not act that way. You still can't ask a boy for a date or propose marriage or kiss him first. No, the new clothes are not the result of *our* sexual freedom. They reflect more than ever that we are still sexual objects for men.

In the past, men fussed over their appearances as much as women. Among the Greeks, the ideal beauty was male; among many primitive tribes, it's the men who wear the beads and feathers; in the great courts of the East and the West, men wore nearly as many frills, perfumes, and wigs as women did. But around the 1830s, Western men seem to have gotten bored with keeping up elaborate appearances and gave up bright clothes, jewelry, and hairpieces for simple, comfortable suits and short, unset hair. The whole burden of beauty was shifted to us, and it's just too much for one sex to have to bear. Let *them* go back to being nervous about the shape of their legs and give *us* time to think about other things for a change.

But aside from the pain, the burden, and the bother, a lot of psychological damage is caused by this business of only the lovely are loved.

If you're not lovely, you get the feeling no one will ever love you.

If you are lovely, you get the feeling that what you are as a person doesn't matter, that men want you only because you have a pretty face or figure.

As we mentioned before, you learn to fear getting older because you may lose your beauty, and then, once again, no one will love you.

And you spend all of your life depending like a child on other people's opinion of you, instead of your opinion of yourself. You don't enjoy your accomplishments as a man does; your pride is centered in your physical being. A man is judged by the work he does. If he does not work, the choice is (usually) his. But the world judges you by your face. And if it isn't pretty, there's nothing you can do about it.

It's too bad that our society discourages girls from reaching for a glory that lasts and encourages them instead to reach for beauty—which doesn't last. And the beauty game is a piece of insanity anyway, because the truth is that men are just as beautiful as women.

There's no reason not to be attractive and enjoy an appreciative glance from a man. There's no reason why a man shouldn't be attractive and enjoy an appreciative glance from a woman. But the burden of having to be the "beautiful" sex, the silliness of having to hide our intelligence behind sexy clothes, and the childishness of having to depend on other people for our sense of worth is a sad and often tragic business.

Men may prefer to keep women in the position of pretty idiots, but women are beginning to prefer not to be kept in that position.

The Happy Housewife

All across America, millions of women make the beds, shop for groceries, do the family wash, chauffeur their children, cook the dinner, sew their husbands' buttons, and they do it all whether they work or not and whether they like it or not. What's more, they're supposed to do it with a smile, because, as John Stuart Mill said in 1860, "All men . . . desire to have, in the woman most nearly connected with them, not a forced slave but a willing one."

Learning to salute the master starts young.

Remember? You're to understand *his* interests come first. You learn not to win the tennis match (high school debate, better grades, and when you get older, higher salaries, job promotions, political arguments) against him—ever. It's natural for him to win, of course. He's been brought up to win. But if you do it, if you win or accomplish anything worthwhile, you've had it. Winning may make the human part of you feel great, but the *feminine* part of you, the part of you that's been brought up to play the female role, ends up feeling like some kind of freak. The boys look at you as if you're strange and, sadly, so do many girls. A good woman slave is supposed to follow her master, not beat him to the draw. (What's awful is that every time you give up or lose on purpose you betray yourself, you lose a little more self-respect and respect for all other women. Losers end up hating themselves and other losers.) But no matter what names you call yourself for giving in all the time, you go on doing it. After all, you've been programmed like a computer to do it.

So why should anything change when you get married? You've been brought up to please a man, to do what he wants. And what a man generally wants is somebody else to wash his socks for him.

He doesn't want you to win the rewards the world has to offer; *he* is your reward. He doesn't want you to earn real money (a little on the side to help the family budget is okay); *he* wants to control the money. He doesn't want you to have the pleasure of standing on your own two feet and feeling like a competent adult; he wants you to stand on his feet so he can choose the direction for both of you. He doesn't want an equal, he wants a worshiper.

The bait for the master-slave trap is that he will take care of you. But why does he have to? You're not a cripple and you're not a child, but you are often brought up to believe you are both. So when the great, big man comes along and says he will take care of you, you give up your life, your career, your sense of satisfaction in yourself, and slide gratefully into his arms with a sigh of relief.

If you're lucky, maybe he will turn out to be strong like your daddy was and gentle and loving like your mommy was, and you can spend the rest of your life snuggling in his arms like a baby. (What you may not find out until afterward, is that, like many men, he is simply an overgrown baby boy, as many girls are overgrown baby girls, and you may be the one who has to come up with the unexpected strength.)

And then, of course, for the first ten years or so of your marriage, you may be so busy with babies that you won't have time to think about much of anything.

Not until the babies grow up and go off to school—will there be plenty of time to think. Then there will be empty hour after empty hour after empty hour of time.

Then it may at last occur to you that as wonderful as your husband may be, there is one thing nobody can take care of for someone else. And that is, the sense of one's own worth. And what is it worth, in the long run, to have the cleanest kitchen floor in the neighborhood?

How often have you heard women say, "I am proud to be a housewife, I am happy being a housewife, I think woman's true role in life is to be a housewife"?

It is true that some people, both men and women, are happy devoting their lives to housekeeping and child care. But that the housewife role is *not* enough for *most* women is proved by the many mental health surveys that have been done. The inferior role given to women in marriage has its effect. Overall, more married than single women are reported to be passive, phobic (afraid of things), and depressed. Almost three times as many married as single women show severe neurotic symptoms. Many more women are in psychotherapy than men. Many more women report their marriages as unhappy than men. Twice as many married women as married men have felt that they were going to have a nervous breakdown. Many more women than men experience psychological and physical anxiety.

Men often say that the reason for women's psychological

problems is that women are more emotionally unstable than men, that we are somehow just "crazier" than they are. This is ridiculous. Any group of people that has suffered oppression, prejudice, discrimination, that has been made to feel inferior, that is not allowed to succeed, that is not allowed the satisfaction of full participation in the world's affairs, that is hardly even permitted to win an argument—is going to suffer psychologically for it. Unfair treatment makes the soul rebel—and if there is no way it can strike back at the world, it will turn the anger inward. And that's what sadness and depression usually are—simply anger turned inward. Women, therefore, are born no more neurotic than men; they're just treated worse.

Why do so many women say they are happy, then, to be somebody's wife and somebody's mother, but never somebody themselves? How does a girl who has been a fast runner, a good math student, someone who draws well or writes well or who has had dreams of becoming a dancer or a designer or a doctor or a teacher—how does such a girl suddenly turn into a woman who is deliriously thrilled to be stuck with the dishes, the laundry, and the company of nothing but an undersized population all day? (I know bringing up children is an important job. But it takes *two* people to make a child, so why should the whole responsibility for care always be a woman's?)

The reason women take all this on and then declare themselves happy to boot is that we have been taught to believe that this is what society expects from us. For some people there is a certain satisfaction in doing, not what they want, but what is expected of them, what they are told is their duty. And then they interpret this as happiness.

Listening to women who call themselves "happy housewives" is oftentimes a little like watching birds whose wings have been clipped. Some women do like it, or adjust to it, but many go on making heartbreaking attempts to fly all their lives.

In the past, when there were no other roads a woman could take, there was some defense for trying to accept things as they were and adjusting to the role of housewife. Healthy people do bow to the unchangeable. When there were no pills or other contraceptive methods so that women were pregnant a lot of the time, when there was no bread in stores so that women had to spend hours doing their own baking, when women had no legal rights, when nobody would give a woman a job, when women aged early and died young from too much work and too much childbearing, when, in many parts of the world, men bought and sold women as slaves, prostitutes, or concubines— there often was no choice but to submit to one's fate and be grateful it was no worse.

But now that women have more rights, now that the doors have been opened (the doors get stuck from time to time when a male foot gets planted firmly on the other side—but they can be opened if a few women get together and give a good, hard shove), now that it is possible to expand our lives, there is no longer any necessity to settle for a new vacuum cleaner as the high point of one's existence.

Yet many women, untrained for independence and pro- grammed only for wifehood and motherhood, go on accepting an inferior, dependent role, go on accepting the depression that comes first when they are trapped in their homes and after- ward when their children grow up and they find nothing to do in their empty nests. They never discover how joyous and ex- citing a relationship between a man and a woman can be when they share not only their bodies but their minds, when the two face each other as equals instead of playing the game (often not even true) of big-man-little-woman.

There is an old saying that a man divides his time between his work and his marriage, while for a woman, marriage is her whole life. A pretty unfair arrangement, but it can be stopped. No man is going to give up his work or his outside interests to even the score. So it remains for a woman to work or have outside interests.

Some women say, "I haven't got time to do anything else. The house keeps me busy from morning till night."

Betty Friedan, who wrote a book called *The Feminine Mystique,* discovered something interesting when she interviewed housewives around the country. She discovered that housework expands to fill whatever time you want to give to it. Women who worked and who only gave a few hours a week to their housework kept their houses just as clean, enjoyed meals just as well cooked, and set up a household routine just as smooth as housewives who stayed home. They didn't change their sheets five times a week or scrub a floor that didn't need scrubbing or bake bread they didn't need just to fill the hours of the day.

Some housewives say, "I don't feel I have any right to complain. Housework may be boring, but my husband's job is just as boring." Maybe, but he's being paid for it!

No matter which way you look at it, for most women, housewifing is simply not enough and not rewarding enough to fill a lifetime. And more and more women are coming to accept this. Alone in the kitchen is a place more and more women don't want to stay.

Section Two

HOW WE GOT THIS WAY

Adam and Eve

Young men and women in schools, colleges, and universities all over the world are fighting today against being limited to traditional sex roles.

Girls have begun to reject being trained to be servants, and boys have begun to reject being trained to be money machines.

Today's students, male and female alike, value individual self-fulfillment. Both sexes encourage each other to do their own thing. Accomplishment is beginning to be no longer limited to the male. And both sexes, not just females, are learning to value the warmth of human relationships. If independence and serious commitment are good values, they are good values for women as well as men. If sensitivity and emotional warmth are good values, they are good values not only for women but for men as well.

In many young marriages, both the man and the woman have jobs or professions, and both share equally the cooking and household chores. The Me-Tarzan-I-Bring-Home-the-Meat-You-Jane-You-Cook-the-Meat recipe for marriage, the breadwinner-homemaker image of the married couple, is fading.

But it isn't fading without a struggle. We have been propagandized for too many thousands of years. And some parents are still rearing their children to fit the popular stereotypes. Think, for a moment, about what ideas you've been brought up on, and how early in life you were fed those ideas.

Think, for a moment, of the Bible.

"In the beginning God created the heavens and the earth. . . . Then God said, Let us make man in our image, after our likeness; and let them have dominion . . . over all the earth . . . and the rib which the Lord God had taken from the man he made into a woman and brought her to the man. . . . Then the Lord God said to the woman, What is this that you have done? The woman said, The serpent beguiled me, and I ate. . . . To the woman He said, I will greatly multiply your pain in child-bearing; in pain you shall bring forth children, yet your desire shall be for your husband, and he shall rule over you." (Genesis 1,2,3.)

St. Paul seconds the motion about who is to rule over whom, and whose is the greater glory.

"For a man ought not to cover his head, since he is the image and glory of God; but woman is the glory of man. For man was not made from woman, but woman from man. Neither was man created for woman, but woman for man." (Corinthians 1:11.)

If the Christians taught male superiority, the Jews were no better. So lowly did they think the status of women, that one Orthodox Jewish prayer goes like this:

Blessed art Thou, oh Lord our God, King of the Universe, that I was not born a gentile.

Blessed art Thou, oh Lord our God, King of the Universe, that I was not born a slave.

Blessed art Thou, oh Lord our God, King of the Universe, that I was not born a woman.

And in the Moslem Koran:

"Men are superior to women on account of the qualities in which God has given them preeminence."

Clearly, it has never occurred to men that another interpretation of the story of Adam and Eve is possible. When God began creating things, he created them in the order of their importance, saving his greatest creation until last. When men tell the story of creation, they talk of Adam as being the highest of God's creations, and Eve as an afterthought. But since, in actual sequence, Eve was the last to be created, why not think of *her* as the crowning achievement of God's creativity?

And as for the business with the apple, men have always ignored its significance. Disobedient or not, it was Eve who took the first bite, and thereby she became the person who brought knowledge into the world.

The myth of male superiority has been taught in many ways and enforced for thousands of years. Ever since our ancestors lived in caves and men decided they were superior because they had more muscles, they have cowed women into submission and believed that men were a higher order of being.

The Greeks had a myth, "Pandora's Box," in which it was said that a woman was responsible for all the suffering in the world. Two of the greatest Greek thinkers, Plato and Aristotle, had horrid things to say about women. Plato was so convinced of all women's lack of intelligence that he wasn't sure they shouldn't be classed as animals. Aristotle went so far as to suggest women might have been born by mistake. Another Greek,

Menander, said, "A woman is necessarily an evil, but he that gets the most tolerable one is lucky."

Orthodox Jews considered women unclean.

Early Christians were taught by St. Paul, "It is not good for a man to touch a woman." They were told by St. Augustine that a woman was like a temple built over a sewer.

Moslems were told by Mohammed that "When Eve was created, Satan rejoiced."

Hindus were told, "A woman must never be free of subjugation."

Since people today are still being taught to read (without questioning the images presented) the writings of the Greek philosophers, and the great religious writings of the past, is it any wonder that the status of women has greatly suffered because of it?

By the Middle Ages, Western churchmen were arguing over whether women even had souls. The church, as well as society, had become completely male dominated, and the Protestant Reformation, when it came along in the sixteenth century, did nothing to help.

Martin Luther believed not only that women were secondary to men, but that sexuality was Original Sin. John Calvin said woman's only useful function was to bear children, and he spoke out against political equality for women.

The great poet John Milton called women a "defect of nature."

For centuries, there were brutal attacks on women who were thought to be in league with the devil. Such women were burned at the stake. Even the great military leader Joan of Arc was burned for being a heretic. She would never have been burned if she had been a man.

In the eighteenth century, during the period of Enlightenment, men were still writing horrid things about women. They may have formulated ideas of freedom for themselves, but they did nothing to release women from bondage.

The French philosopher Rousseau wrote that it was necessary to discipline women so that they would be obedient to men. He said it was "necessary to accustom them early to such confinement, that it may not afterward cost them too dear; and to the suppression of their caprices that they may the more readily submit to the will of others." He also wrote, "She ought to learn even to suffer injustices and to bear the insults of a husband without complaint."

Diderot, another French philosopher, wrote, "Women prefer lustful, depraved men because women are depraved and lustful."

Lord Chesterfield, a famous woman-hater, wrote advice to his son.

Women, then, are only children of a larger growth; they have an entertaining tattle, and sometimes wit; but for solid reasoning, good sense, I never knew in my life one that had it. . . . A man of sense only trifles with them, plays with them, humors and flatters them . . . but he neither consults them about, nor trusts them with serious matters. . . . Women have in truth but two passions, vanity and love; these are their universal characters.

Even the great American liberal Thomas Jefferson said in 1807, "The appointment of a woman to office is an innovation for which the public is not prepared—nor am I."

The poet Tennyson wrote, "Woman is the lesser man."

George Meredith: "I expect that Woman will be the last thing civilized by Man."

Schopenhauer called women "childish, frivolous, and short-sighted."

Nietzsche said, "When you go to a woman, do not forget to take along your whip." It was in Hitler's Germany that modern woman-hating was the worst. Hitler even declared that woman's emancipation was a Jewish plot. The Nazi movement was declared to be a masculine movement, and women were denied voting rights and the right to hold public office. They were told their only acceptable activities were children, kitchen, and church.

In the early part of this century, Alfred Adler, a Viennese psychiatrist wrote, "All our institutions, our traditional attitudes, our laws, our morals, our customs, give evidence of the fact that they are determined and maintained by the privileged males for the glory of male domination. . . . They believe that women are here only for the purpose of being submissive."

Although it is quite true that laws and customs and values are changing, that people are beginning to understand that just because men have muscles it doesn't give them the right to rule over women (and those muscles are about as useful in our modern push-button society as an appendix), and although our twentieth century democratic philosophies have developed new ideas about the equality of every human being, it's still going to take a while to change things.

The Bound Foot

For about 2 million years, human beings lived by hunting and gathering their food. The men hunted wild animals, and the women gathered wild berries, fruits, nuts, roots, eggs, and insects.

Tarzanists believe that in those early times the women and children spent their days lolling about the cave waiting for the big man to come home from his dangerous and exhausting hunt with the bacon. George Bernard Shaw put these words into the mouth of Cain in his play *Back to Methuselah:*

I will hunt: I will fight and strive to the very bursting of my sinews. When I have slain the boar at the risk of my life, I will throw it to the woman to cook, and give her a morsel of it for her pains. She shall have no other food, and that will make her my slave. . . . Man shall be the master of Woman.

This is, of course, all absolute nonsense. It was never like that, and among surviving hunting communities it is not like that now. Studies of primitive peoples in the Kalahari Desert of Africa show that hunting is often slow and unpredictable, and that vegetable foods gathered by the women comprise from 60 to 80 percent of the total diet of everyone. Outside the Arctic, this 60 to 80 percent holds true for all hunting-gathering groups studied to date.

Women in primitive societies were of primary economic importance. It is generally accepted now that, owing to her ancient role as the gatherer of vegetable foods, woman was responsible for the invention and development of agriculture. The invention of agriculture about 10,000 years ago was an important revolution, because with food readily available there was time to improve tools, invent handwriting, and develop all the arts and sciences that made for civilization. The women of the New Stone Age, because they brought forth food from the earth and children from their bodies, were worshipped and given status, as the widespread remains of shrines and the clay statues of the Mother Goddess from Southwest Asia to Europe prove. Anthropologists have discovered that in many non-Western cultures—among the Hopi Indians; in Burma, Indonesia, and in certain African tribes below the Sahara—women have had more freedom and equality than in the more technologically advanced civilizations of Asia, Europe, and the United States.

Although women played so great a part in producing civilization, their status changed with the coming of male rulers and priests, with city living, and military conquests. Records show that even in the great early civilizations of Egypt, Babylonia, Greece, Rome, India, China, and Japan, men dominated women, treated them as property, and used them mainly for childbearing or for pleasure. From that time on the position of women varied little, until the late nineteenth century.

Not only have women in major civilizations had no political rights; not only have they been ranted at by orators and writers who called them inferiors, animals, mindless, and the source of sin; not only have they attained rights and then had them taken away again; not only all this, but they have suffered physical bondage and punishment as well.

For a thousand years, up to early days of this century, Chinese girls had their feet bound in childhood, at six or seven years of age. Lengths of bandage were wrapped around the four smaller toes and the heel, very tightly, in order to bend the toes under the foot and make the arch high and bowed. An ideal foot was three inches long. To attain this, little girls suffered intense pain. Pus and blood often dripped from their bandages, their toes broke. And once their feet were bound they were never able to run about. In fact, girls and women could barely hobble around; they had to use walls, canes, and the support of others even to move about the house. A Chinese woman's life was spent modestly concealed indoors, and if she went out, she went in a curtained sedan chair. Although this crippling device was supposed to make the woman beautiful, a Chinese manual gives a more practical purpose. "Why are feet bound? It is not because they are good looking with their bowed arch, but rather because men feared that women might easily leave their quarters and therefore had their feet bound tightly in order to prevent this." In China, women were often a man's property, bought as concubines or slaves. A man did not want the chastity of his property damaged, so he made certain his women could not move very far.

In Moslem countries, for centuries women were confined to harems, or women's apartments. The women were veiled and kept in strict seclusion from the world. A man might have four wives and as many concubines as he could afford; his power over them was absolute. In some Arab countries, women are still bought and sold into harems, and a man's power over the lives of women in his harem is still absolute.

In some African tribes, women were castrated (their clitorises cut off) to prevent them from feeling sexual pleasure.

Forceful restraint and punishment of women was not confined to the East and Near East. When medieval knights went off to war, they had a habit of locking chastity belts around the waists and between the legs of their wives in order to ensure that they behaved properly while their men were away. Physical punishment then was also perfectly legal. Church law permitted husbands to beat their women with whips and sticks (not, however, with iron weapons).

The ancient Hebrews sold their daughters into marriage. Babylonians auctioned off women to the highest bidders. In ancient Greece, Athenian women were confined to their homes. Not only could they not vote, they could not even appear in the streets. (In Sparta, women were a little better off. They could own land. On occasion, they even had two husbands.) In ancient Rome, women had rights over their own property, but men had the power of life and death over the women.

Christians borrowed the Hebrew attitude toward women and gradually took away what few rights the Roman women had gained. The jurists of the Middle Ages made a pronouncement that women could have no personal identity, and in England it was "adjudged that the wife has nothing of her own while her husband lives."

Men throughout the ages who possessed unusual wisdom were called prophets, seers, philosophers. Women who possessed unusual wisdom or who dared to be different were generally called witches, and in the seventeenth century especially, many such women in Europe and America were hanged or burned at the stake.

For thousands of years, especially in the Near East and Far East, though it happened in Europe too, families could sell their daughters as prostitutes into brothels or as slaves. Selling females, legally or not, is still practiced in some parts of the world. Selling girls and women into brothels was even done in Victorian England, less than a hundred years ago, and in America. In the early part of this century, especially, white slavery flourished. And the viciousness with which black women were treated in all areas where black slavery flourished is among the greatest horrors of Western history.

It's true that throughout history, there have been great women. There have been great rulers like Cleopatra of Egypt, Elizabeth and Victoria of England, Catherine of Russia, and various empresses of China and Japan. Thousands of women have been important powers behind the political scene. There have been important women writers, important women scientists, important women in religion. The trouble is, that for all their importance, they made no permanent difference in women's rights. Give or take a few primitive societies, women until this century have remained dominated and subjugated by men.

The Empty Mind

Throughout history, we have lacked most of the legal rights of men. We have lacked political representation. We have been confined, sold, and mutilated. Even when we have been treated well, we have been thought of as children, not adults.

A question that is often raised is, "Well, if women were so discontented with their lot, why didn't they strike out on their own?"

The answer to that is, "With what!"

The most important tool for getting anywhere in this world, aside from personal freedom, is training, or education.

While it is true that in most civilizations, many women of the upper classes were taught to read and write, in the past women in general had little or no education at all. Even among the upper classes, women's education was confined primarily to such feminine arts as embroidery, a little singing, the playing of a musical instrument, or dabbling in art. Women were seldom taught anything they could use to make a living. They were even advised that it was unfeminine to do any one thing very well.

Mrs. Ellis gave exactly that warning to young women in her book *The Family Monitor and Domestic Guide,* which was widely read in England and the United States in the middle of the nineteenth century.

> It must not be supposed that the writer is one who would advocate as essential to woman, any very extraordinary degree of intellectual attainment, especially if confined to one particular branch of study. . . . To be able to do a great many things tolerably well, is of infinitely more value to a woman, than to be able to excel in any one.

It was simply not ladylike to draw attention to oneself by doing anything very well.

St. Paul said women should listen in silence and be taught by their husbands—but he meant their duty, not science and mathematics.

In the nineteenth century, Rousseau belittled women's intellectual abilities. "Almost all of them learn with reluctance to read and write; but very readily apply themselves to the use of their needles." He felt that it was useless to teach women to think because their minds were unfit for abstract thought, and that women's entire education ought to be confined to learning to please men.

It was even thought that women's brains were smaller in relation to their size than men's brains and therefore less able. Alexander Walker wrote about beauty in women in 1837 and concluded that the ideal beauty's head ought to be small "because the mental system in the female ought to be subordinate to the vital."

There is a German proverb that says: "A woman has the form of an angel . . . and the mind of an ass."

It was thought that an intellectual woman was unfeminine. Nietzsche said, "When a woman inclines to learning there is usually something wrong with her sex apparatus."

Lady Mary Wortley Montagu advised her daughter to hide her learning "like a physical defect."

So because men thought we had inferior minds to begin with, and because they felt threatened by intelligent women, women were simply left uneducated for anything but household work and motherhood and a little graceful dabbling on the side.

Latourette says of the education of Chinese women up until this century that while many in wealthy families were given some tutoring, most women were illiterate. Girls were primarily educated in the management of a household, in ceremonial duties, in courtesy, and in the proprieties. Women's sphere was believed to be the home. (To underscore the fact that it was our oppression, not our faculties, that were at fault, in two countries where women were most confined, in China and in the Arab countries, women often ran brisk businesses from their homes and hid the proceeds from their husbands.)

In Europe, too, women were barred from all but the most elementary of education. The girls of better families were taught to read and write, but were refused entrance into all institutions of higher learning. An exceptional woman might have herself tutored or teach herself more than was usual, but this was rare.

Occasionally a lonely woman raised a voice in protest. Lady Winchilsea, a seventeenth-century Englishwoman wrote:

> How are we fallen! Fallen by mistaken rules
> And Education's more than Nature's fools;

> Debarred from all improvements of the mind
> And to be dull, expected and designed
> And if some one would soar above the rest,
> With warmer fancy and ambitions pressed,
> So strong the opposing faction still appears,
> The hopes to thrive can ne'er outweigh the fears.

Not only did women remain uneducated, but those few who did manage to use their intellects were shamed, made to feel unwomanly and afraid of criticism.

It was toward the end of the eighteenth century that the protest to free women and to give them an education began to grow. It is hardly a coincidence that the struggle to free women began in America just after the Revolutionary War and grew strong at the time of the Civil War when women helped fight to free the slaves.

Thomas Paine, spokesman for the Revolution, was among the first to condemn, in 1775, the position of women. He said, "even in countries where they may be esteemed the most happy, [women are] . . . robbed of freedom and will by the laws, the slaves of opinion."

Mary Wollstonecraft, who spearheaded the feminist movement in England, said in 1792 that it was hardly surprising that women concentrated on the way they looked instead of what was in their minds since not much had been put into their minds to begin with.

In America ten years earlier, Judith Sargent Murray said women needed knowledge to envision new goals and grow by reaching for them.

Finally, there was a coeducational college—Oberlin, founded in 1832, in Ohio. But even at Oberlin, the administrators decided women's minds couldn't cope with the same courses as men, and they were given a special literary course. The great feminist Lucy Stone, who attended Oberlin, wrote:

> Oberlin's attitude was that women's high calling was to be
> the mothers of the race. . . . If women became lawyers,

ministers, physicians, lecturers, politicians or any sort of "public character," the home would suffer from neglect.
. . .

Washing the men's clothes, caring for their rooms, serving them at table, listening to their orations, but themselves remaining respectfully silent in public assemblages, the Oberlin "co-eds" were being prepared for intelligent motherhood and a properly subservient wifehood.

Lucy Stone had been inspired to seek an education for herself when she heard Mary Lyon speak of education for women at a church sewing circle. Mary Lyon had been traveling all through New England collecting money in order to found a woman's college. She started Mount Holyoke, which, in 1837, opened its doors to give women their first chance at education equal to a man's. The women learned mathematics, the sciences, history, philosophy—not how to be better wives and mothers. Because women were not admitted to the great men's universities, toward the end of the century more women's colleges were founded—Vassar, Smith, Wellesley, Bryn Mawr.

Women—and even a few men who realized that half the human race was being denied the right to become fully human—had finally begun to fight the conditions that had enslaved them for centuries, the conditions summed up by the first Woman's Rights Convention in Seneca Falls, New York, in 1848. The women said of man:

He has compelled her to submit to laws in the formation of which she has no voice. . . . He has made her, if married, in the eyes of the law, civilly dead. He has taken from her all right to property, even to the wages she earns. . . . He closes against her all the avenues of wealth and distinction which he considers most honorable to himself. . . . He has denied her the facilities for obtaining a thorough education, all colleges being closed against her.

But when we got our own colleges at last, there were still more steps to be taken. Without the right to vote, women still had no real power. As M. Carey Thomas, the brilliant first president of Bryn Mawr, said in 1908:

> Women are one-half the world, but until a century ago . . . women lived a twilight life, a half life apart, and looked out and saw men as shadows walking. It was a man's world. The laws were men's laws, the government a man's government, the country a man's country. Now women have won the right to higher education and economic independence. The right to become citizens of the state is the next and inevitable consequence of education and work outside the home. We have gone so far; we must go farther. We cannot go back.

The right to education was the first necessity. The feminists of the last century who fought for women's rights to higher education, careers, the vote, understood that it was necessary to shatter the image of woman as a silly, useless decoration, as a passive, mindless animal, as someone incapable of making her own decisions about her life. It had to be proved that women were fully human. It had to be proved that women needed a sense of their own identity, as men had always had. It had to be proved that women were the equals of men. And for that education was essential.

Yet there are still people who question the "fitness" of fully educating women. There are still men—and women!—who think of girls as feeble-minded creatures whose only destiny is to breed babies. These are the people who want to prevent women from taking full part in the shaping of the world, who still insist that women are "outsiders."

There was a play, written by Henrik Ibsen, in 1879, called *A Doll's House*. Women in Europe and America for nearly a hundred years have identified themselves with Nora, the heroine, when they hear her say:

> You have always been so kind to me. But our home has been nothing but a playroom. I have been your doll wife,

just as at home I was Papa's doll child; and here the children have been my dolls. I thought it great fun when you played with me, just as they thought it fun when I played with them. That is what our marriage has been, Torvald. . . .

How am I fitted to bring up the children? . . . There is another task I must undertake first. I must try and educate myself—you are not the man to help me in that. I must do that for myself. And that is why I am going to leave you now. . . . I must stand quite alone if I am to understand myself and everything about me. It is for that reason that I cannot remain with you any longer.

Torvald is horrified that Nora is leaving him and reminds her that before all else she is a wife and mother. Nora answers:

I believe that before all else I am a reasonable human being, just as you are—or, at all events, that I must try and become one.

Indeed, before all else we must make of ourselves reasonable human beings.

The Feminist Struggle

In a discussion with a group of teenage girls on the subject of women's liberation I said, "The aim of American feminism is the overthrow of the most rigid class system in existence, the class system based on sex."

One of the girls nodded in happy approval and then said, "What I don't understand is why it took women so long to decide to fight back."

The answer is that until the Industrial Revolution in the nineteenth century, it was impossible for most women, no matter how free they wished to be, to find work that would allow them to be financially independent of men. Until the nineteenth century, all circumstances combined to keep even the few educated women at home. Society urgently needed women to bear children and did everything it could to make sure women did just that.

It took the Industrial Revolution with its growth of factories —and because of the factories, the need for a larger work force—to create enough jobs for women. And then it took, in this century, the discovery of effective methods of birth control, to free us from constant pregnancy. It is necessary, in order to fight for freedom, to be able to earn your own living and to be in a position to control your own body.

It was in the middle of the nineteenth century, with industrialization in full swing, that the first full-fledged feminist movement got underway. It's not surprising that the active struggle for women's freedom began in America. We were a young country, less bound by tradition than other lands. We had just come through the American Revolution, with its ideals of freedom. We were confronted with the Civil War and the abolitionist struggle to free the slaves. Freedom was in the air, and American women began to decide they wanted it for themselves.

It was in the cause of antislavery that women first got together politically. In 1837, the year Mount Holyoke opened, American women held their first national antislavery convention in New York. Then in 1840, Elizabeth Cady Stanton (on her honeymoon) and Lucretia Mott (mother of five), met in London at an antislavery convention. When they arrived, Mott, Stanton, and the rest of the delegation of American women were barred from taking part in the convention and were shut off behind a curtain in the back gallery. At that point, the women decided it wasn't only the slaves that needed to be freed.

Eight years later, in 1848, Mott and Stanton organized the first convention on women's rights in Seneca Falls. The Seneca Falls Declaration was modeled on the Declaration of Independence and lists the grievances and sufferings of women everywhere.

The history of mankind is a history of repeated injuries and usurpations on the part of man toward woman, having in direct object the establishment of an absolute tyranny over her. . . .

He has never permitted her to exercise her inalienable right to the elective franchise.

He has compelled her to submit to laws in the formation of which she had no voice.

He has withheld from her rights which are given to the most ignorant and degraded men—both natives and foreigners.

Having deprived her of this first right of a citizen . . . he has oppressed her on all sides.

He has made her, if married, in the eye of the law, civilly dead.

He has taken from her all right in property, even to the wages she earns.

. . . she is compelled to promise obedience to her husband, he becoming to all intents and purposes, her master —the law giving him power to deprive her of her liberty and to administer chastisement.

He has so framed the laws of divorce, as to what shall be the proper causes, and in case of separation, to whom the guardianship of the children shall be given, as to be wholly regardless of the happiness of women—the law, in all cases, going upon a false supposition of the supremacy of man, and giving all power into his hands.

After depriving her of all rights as a married woman, if single and the owner of property, he has taxed her. . . .

He has monopolized nearly all the profitable employments. . . . He closes against her all the avenues to wealth and distinction. . . .

He has denied her the facilities for obtaining a thorough education, all colleges being closed against her.

There were more grievances on women's lack of place in religion, their persecution morally under the double standard, the inferior and abject life they were forced to lead, and they insisted "that they have immediate admission to all the rights and privileges which belong to them as citizens of the United States."

The newspapers ridiculed the women of Seneca Falls and called them aged spinsters who could not find husbands. But despite the ridicule and the name calling, in the years that followed, women's rights conventions and meetings were held throughout the country. And here and there, they received male support. In Boston, in 1853, the Reverend Theodore Parker preached: "To make one-half the human race consume its energies in the functions of housekeeper, wife and mother is a monstrous waste of the most precious material God ever made."

Despite the opposition they faced, many women went on struggling for the right to vote. They lobbied, lectured, held parades, demonstrated, and gathered petitions in their effort to introduce suffrage for women into Congress. Antifeminists called them unnatural, man-eating monsters and reported them as big, mannish women who smoked cigars and swore like troopers. It was true many of the early feminists cut their hair short and wore bloomers and tried to be like men. Why not? They saw the pitiable lives their mothers led and had every reason to reject the traditional image of women.

Lucy Stone, who, with Elizabeth Cady Stanton and Susan B. Anthony, was among the foremost leaders of the women's rights movement, was a small, feminine woman with a gentle voice. She lectured on abolition Saturdays and Sundays, as an agent for the Anti-Slavery Society, and during the rest of the week, on women's rights. Although she was described as "a prototype of womanly grace," men threatened her with clubs, threw eggs at her, and once in the middle of winter, pushed a hose through a window and sprayed her with icy water. Although Lucy Stone had said, "Marriage is to a woman a state of slavery," she did finally marry. But she and her husband agreed to a special pact at the ceremony—there was to be no vow of obedience and no superiority on the part of the husband. Afterward, Lucy Stone kept her own name, in fear that to become a wife was to die as a person.

Susan B. Anthony, brilliant leader of the suffrage movement, never married, but devoted her life to the cause. She declared,

> By law, public sentiment and religion from the time of Moses down to the present day, woman has never been thought of other than as a piece of property, to be disposed of at the will and pleasure of man. Women must be educated out of their unthinking acceptance of financial dependence on man into mental and economic independence. [Women must not] sell themselves—in marriage or out—for bread and shelter.

When men scoffed at the suffragists and said women had it easy because men were so chivalrous toward them, Elizabeth Cady Stanton (who wrote a *Woman's Bible* to disprove what she considered misinterpretations about women in the Bible) was outraged. She said,

> Talk not to us of chivalry, that died long ago . . . a man in love will jump to pick up a glove or bouquet for a silly girl of sixteen, whilst at home he will permit his aged mother to carry pails of water and armfuls of wood or his wife to lug a twenty-pound baby, hour after hour, without ever offering to relieve her.

Angelina Grimké, another great fighter for women's rights answered the question of chivalry this way. "I ask no favors for my sex. I surrender not our claim to equality. All I ask of our brethren is that they will take their feet from off our necks and permit us to stand upright on the ground which God has designed us to occupy!"

Alice Stone Blackwell, Lucy Stone's daughter, remarked, "Justice is better than chivalry if we cannot have both."

But it was Sojourner Truth—who had been born into slavery, was freed, and, along with Harriet Tubman, went back time and again with a huge price on her head to free other slaves—who made perhaps the most moving statement of all when men talked about how chivalrous they were toward the "frailty" of women.

> The man over there says women need to be helped into carriages and lifted over ditches, and to have the best places everywhere. Nobody ever helps me into carriages, or over puddles, or gives me the best place—and ain't I a woman? Look at my arm! I have ploughed and planted and gathered into barns and no man could head me—and ain't I a woman? I could work as much and eat as much as a man—when I could get it—and bear the lash as well! And ain't I a woman? I have borne thirteen children, and seen most of 'em sold into slavery, and when I cried out with my mother's grief, none but Jesus heard me—and ain't I a woman?

The sad part of the early feminist struggle was that while the battle to free the slaves was being won, the battle for women's rights got nowhere. Sojourner Truth said, "There is a great stir about colored men getting their rights, but not a word about colored women; and if colored men get their rights, and not colored women theirs, you see the colored men will be masters over the women, and it will be just as bad as it was before."

It was true for white women as well.

When the war was over, the black men got the vote. But not the black women. Nor the white women, either.

During their lifetimes, the pioneer feminists saw the laws of almost every state change toward women: high schools opened to them, and two-thirds of the colleges in the United States. But it took another generation to finish the battle for woman's vote.

As the fight to free women was spurred on by the fight to free slaves in the nineteenth century, so in the twentieth century it was spurred on by the fight for social reform. The new feminists fought against the horrible working conditions in factories, against child labor, and for the rise of unions.

The final battle for the vote was led by Carrie Chapman Catt, a teacher and a newspaper woman. In 1913, tens of thousands of suffragists marched in torchlight parades in New York, Boston, Chicago, and Washington, D.C. In Washington, nearly ten thousand women marched on the White House. The police did nothing while mobs attacked the women, knocking them down, slapping them, throwing burning cigar stubs at them. They were beaten and bloodied and dragged off to hospitals and jails. A group of women who chained themselves to the White House fence were arrested and dragged off to jail. There they went on hunger strikes and were martyred by forced feeding.

While this was happening in America, a similar struggle was going on in other countries. The battle in England was even bloodier than here. Women broke windows, poured acid into mailboxes, and attacked members of Parliament with stones and whips. In return the women were brutally treated in jail.

But despite the hostility they met, the feminists went on fighting and winning adherents. The organizations formed to work for the vote had about 2 million members throughout the country. And at last the effort paid off.

The Nineteenth Amendment to the United States Constitution was signed on August 26, 1920, designed to give 26 million women the right to vote. But even then it took two more years to get the amendment ratified! And it was 1922 before the Supreme Court finally ruled that women could vote.

Carrie Chapman Catt had worked not only for American women. In 1904, she had helped to organize the International Woman Suffrage Alliance, and by 1920, when we won our vote, so had the women of twenty-two other countries.

But with victory, came tragedy. With the winning of the vote, the feminist movement died. Some of the women went on to form the League of Women Voters, but the League can only lobby, not elect. Women had the vote, but they were not elected to office and therefore still did not have an equal voice with men in making the laws of this country.

Most of the suffragists went back to their homes, considering their work done. It was to be another fifty years before the sound of feminism was heard again.

Back to the Cave

A fifty-year silence followed the first great feminist struggle to win the right to vote.

One reason was male backlash. "We gave you the vote," men said, "what more do you want!"

The men of the twenties understood that feminism was a threat to their centuries-old power over women. They may have been forced by the feminists to give women the vote. They even enjoyed some of the new personal freedoms women claimed: shorter skirts, cigarette-smoking ("you've come a long way, baby"), greater sexual freedom, young women around the office instead of male secretaries (now women served men outside the home as well as inside). But the men were not about to give up the real power, either politically or economically, that they had always held.

Another reason we got no further than winning the right to vote was the women themselves. Political muscle is the only true guarantee of equality. Those women who remained active in politics made two enormous mistakes. They did not push for political office themselves, they supported male candidates. And while they continued to fight for human rights—for blacks, for oppressed workers, for victims of Franco's Spain and Hitler's Germany, for child labor laws, for pure food and drug statutes—they stopped fighting for women's rights, considering them all won. They did not understand themselves politically. They thought they were free.

So instead of continuing the fight in the political arena, women reveled in their small, personal freedoms of dress and life style. The few feminists left were ridiculed, women's political consciousness was watered down. Having got the vote, they figured that was all there was to it, and they turned their attention to a personal search for fulfillment instead of laying the groundwork for political and social rights for all women everywhere.

Women had not yet come to realize that to win the battle for civil rights is one thing; to win the battle against prejudice is another.

Okay, we got the vote—but nobody would vote for a woman.

Okay, we got jobs—but we got the worst jobs, the worst pay.

Okay, we got ourselves educated and into the professions, but those first women in business and the professions were thought to be freaks, just as the early feminists were thought to be holy terrors and man-eaters. The result was that a girl growing up had one of two images to choose from: she could either retreat into the narrow-submissive-but-adored wife and mother role, or she could plow forward in her chosen field and risk becoming what everybody thought of career women—if not a man-eating terror, certainly a woman loveless and alone. It wasn't much of a choice, and many girls, understandably, did not see that there was a third choice—becoming a successful human being on all fronts.

Society helped women betray themselves. In the twenties, sexiness was the fashion, and "romance" became entangled with marriage. Everybody wanted to be a gay flapper, a sultry Theda Bara, an adorable Clara Bow, a beautiful and romantic Greta Garbo. The movie-and-magazine emphasis on romantic marriage, on personal style, lured women away from their feminist solidarity with its emphasis on work and independence and back into the shackles of housekeeping. The image of marriage had been glamorized, the Myth of Emancipation was in the air, but the fact was, women's position in society was not much different from before.

In the thirties, the Depression sobered women as well as men. Trying to be Theda Bara obviously wasn't the answer to women's happiness. So instead of flappers, women began to be do-gooders. But they were still miserable, they still weren't fulfilled, and it began to confuse them. They had the vote, they didn't understand what more they needed, and secretly they began to wonder if they were inferior after all.

The early forties helped. With the men away at World War II, women filled many powerful positions and began to feel like human beings instead of second-class citizens. It's a sad commentary that it took a world war to give women a chance. Society genuinely needed women to work to their fullest capacities then, and for the first time many women were given human instead of "female" treatment.

And then two things happened. The men came home from the war to reclaim the jobs and fill the universities (men were still given preference in most places, of course). And the message of Freud and other *male* psychologists and scientists filled the air. Between the age-old prejudices against women as inferiors and the new prejudices formed by the new science of psychology, women were slapped back down all over again.

In the late forties and fifties Freudian thought made a tremendous impact on the American woman. Because Freud was a genius, because he was the founder of psychoanalysis, because it was he who discovered the unconscious workings of the mind, educated people everywhere accepted Freudian truth. No one can question the contribution Freud made to our pursuit of knowledge, to science, to man's understanding of himself. But that's exactly the problem. Freud helped *man* to understand himself—he knew nothing whatever of the psychology of women.

First of all, like most Victorian men, Freud believed a woman's place was in the home, and in the home only. (One would have hoped that Freud had known better, but he was, alas a man, and a nineteenth century European man at that.) In letters he wrote to Martha, his fiancée, during the four years he made her wait before their marriage, Freud said:

"I know, after all, how sweet you are, how you can turn a house into a paradise, how you will share in my interests, how gay yet painstaking you will be. I will let you rule the house as much as you wish. . . ."

Freud spent years telling Martha to be a good little wife and devote her interests only and entirely to *him, his* house, *his* interests. He was convinced it was the only way any woman could be happy. In another letter, on the subject of John Stuart Mill's views on "female emancipation," Freud wrote,

In his whole presentation, it never emerges that women are different beings. . . . It is really a stillborn thought to send women into the struggle of existence exactly as man. If, for instance, I imagined my gentle sweet girl as a competitor, it would only end in my telling her, as I did seventeen months ago, that I am fond of her and that I implore her to withdraw from the strife into the calm, uncompetitive activity of my home. . . . Long before the age at which a man can earn a position in society, Nature has determined woman's destiny through beauty, charm, and sweetness. Law and custom have much to give women that has been withheld from them, but the position of women will surely be what it is: in youth an adored darling and in mature years a loved wife.

"Anatomy is destiny," said Freud. "Women are lesser human beings, childlike dolls; their bodies and minds fit them best for housework and the bearing of children and the service of men. Our ideal of womanhood would be lost, if women were educated to take their places in the world." (Not that Freud thought most women were fit to be educated anyway.)

(Don't forget, as you read this, that people *truly believed* in what Freud had to say!)

Freud stressed the important influence that childhood had on a person's adult years; he said that mature mental health depended to a great extent on what had happened to a person as an infant and child. He was the first to understand that children are sexual beings from the beginning of their lives, and that their early sexual feelings determine a great part of their personalities later on. Freud's theories formed much of the basis of psychoanalysis today, and their brilliance is unquestionable.

In one area, however, he was not only wrong, but he did untold damage. That area was his theories on women. He conceived of an idea he called "penis envy." He believed that women themselves and all men considered females inferior because they don't have penises. He thought that women spent their whole lives wishing they had penises and feeling that people who had them were better than people who didn't. He said that when children discover that girls don't have penises, both boys and girls believe it is because somehow the little girl's penis has been cut off. Both end up thinking of her as a boy-with-something-missing, an inferior being.

(Feminist psychiatrists and many male psychiatrists know now that this is nonsense, that girls feel inferior because society treats them that way, not because they are without penises. After all, boys don't have uteruses, and they don't walk around feeling inferior because they can't produce babies. While it's true that many girls do envy boys or go through periods when they want to be boys, what they envy is not masculine genitalia, but masculine freedom.)

Freud went on to say that because girls felt less well equipped than boys, they often grew up neurotic or with a "masculinity complex." In other words, they tried to be like men. He viewed any woman who wanted to work outside the home, who wanted to follow a profession, who went into business, not as a woman trying to fulfill herself as a person, but as a woman trying to be like a man, a woman pretending to have a penis.

The effect of Freudian thought was exactly what you might expect. For twenty years—and it still goes on—people reversed their attitudes toward the gains the feminists had made. They went back to thinking, as Freud told them, that women were inferior, that they belonged in the home, and that any woman who wanted a career was sick in the head because she was trying to be a man. The prejudice against women grew worse than ever.

Freud's followers, both male and female psychiatrists, didn't help matters at all. Helene Deutsch, Bruno Bettelheim, Erik Erikson, Joseph Reingold—great names in their field—held Freud's views, seeing women as breeders, to be fulfilled only through a husband and children.

Erik Erikson said in 1964,

Much of a young woman's identity is already defined in her kind of attractiveness and in the selectivity of her search for the man." Mature, womanly fulfillment depends on the fact that a woman has an "inner space" destined to bear the offspring of chosen men, and with it, a biological, psychological, and ethical commitment to take care of human infancy.

Bruno Bettelheim (1967):

. . . as much as women want to be good scientists and engineers, they want, first and foremost, to be womanly companions of men and to be mothers.

Joseph Reingold (1969):

. . . woman is nurturance . . . anatomy decrees the life of a woman. When women grow up without dread of their biological functions and without the subversion of feminist doctrine and therefore enter upon motherhood with a sense of fulfillment and altruistic sentiment, we shall attain the goal of a good life and a secure world in which to live.

Even Dr. Spock (1969):

Biologically and temperamentally, I believe, women were made to be concerned first and foremost with child care, husband care and home care.

It makes pretty horrible reading, doesn't it. The tyrannical male psychologists of the world seem to have passed sentence on women everywhere, condemning them to serve men forever (those male psychologists must, of course, find it convenient to have their wives serve them while they continue to do the important work of thinking!)

Happily, the many great women in the Association of Women in Psychology have begun to attack these views and so end such stupid nonsense and such ignorance for all time.

Women didn't get much help from other sciences during these years either. American sociology, during this period, stressed the differing functions of men and women as opposed to the fact that we are all human beings with the right to grow and fulfill ourselves. It was the era of the homemaker-breadwinner recipe for marriage.

In the growing science of anthropology, the situation was no better. As Elaine Morgan points out in her book *The Descent of Woman,* evolutionists were so busy talking about *mankind* and about *man* as the hero of our history (why is it always *his*tory instead of *her*story?), that woman and her contributions to evolution were generally pretty much ignored. As Elaine Morgan says, half of our ancestors were women, which means that half the genes we have inherited belong to women, which further means that half of what men, as well as women, are is directly attributable to women. This is certainly a fact that anthropologists like Robert Ardrey tend to forget. In his *African Genesis,* Ardrey is forever pointing out that it was the males who had instincts for a home, for status, for organization, for order, indeed for just about everything that contributes to the civilizing process. To females he gives only a sexual-and-reproductive instinct. What he is saying, in effect, is that males have made the world what it is.

It would be nice, as Elaine Morgan says, if just once we could read a volume that began, "When the first ancestor of the human race descended from the trees, *she* had not yet developed the mighty brain that was to distinguish her so sharply from all other species. . . ."

While it is perfectly true, then, that after the 1920s we had won a great many rights we had never had before, public opinion was still against us. There is not much point in teaching a girl to do algebra, letting her play baseball, letting her think independently, and giving her a college education if, at the end of all that, everybody says, "Go home and stay there." Voting and the right to an education are all very well, but if scholars tell you that you're a second-class person, a man "with something missing," and that if you leave the house you will never be fulfilled, it can really mess your head up.

It's as if girls were being told: "You can try to do what you want with your life, but if you do, you're sick."

It was a damned-if-you-do, damned-if-you-don't situation.

The Beginning of Success

The general attitudes of society, Freud included, made the
fifties the worst decade for women since the winning of the
vote. Betty Friedan documents it brilliantly in *The Feminine
Mystique*. She calls it the great sellout of American women.
Good Housekeeping, Parents' Magazine, True Confessions
were the Bibles, and their message was that the only true and
happy role for woman was the creative art of washing dishes
and diapers. It wasn't described as one of many possible
choices for women—it was described as the *only* choice. And
if you weren't happy scrubbing floors, you were some kind of
freak. What you got in return for the sadness of discovering
that "romantic marriage" wasn't all it was cracked up to be

were *respectability* and painkillers like Try a New Diet, Try a New Sewing Machine, Try a New Approach to Cooking—or, if you were really going out of your mind—Try a New Psychiatrist.

If the mothers of the fifties were lost and confused, young girls didn't fare much better. Nobody remembered feminism by then. Nobody remembered that to feel like a free human being, you have to act like one. So young women, instead of taking a long, hard look at their mothers' lives and trying to figure out a better way, escaped from their dull homes by following the same path their mothers had—Falling In Love. Only they did it earlier and earlier. What had been reserved for the late teens moved into the early teens. The Parked Car, The Senior Prom, Popularity, The Dating Ritual remained essential rites in the life of a girl. They just started earlier. And still the boys grew up to achieve; the girls, after a brief teenage fling, were sent back into the home.

By the sixties, the boys had had enough of the elongated romantic ritual. They figured there had to be an easier way to get sex. There was. The boys began to leave home in hordes—for Europe, for the Peace Corps, for Greenwich Village, the riots of Berkeley, the civil rights demonstrations in Mississippi, the hippie scene from Haight-Ashbury to the East Village, anywhere away from the controls of parents and a rigid society. And wherever they went, the boys found "groovy chicks" to "swing" with. If the girls didn't want to play, they were called "uptight" and shrugged off. There were plenty of chicks around who were still so anxious for male approval they would live any way the boys wanted them to live. The girls were still afraid to get together and make a stand, and each, in private, still searched for her own private solution.

One of the places in which girls and women began to "do their own thing" was in the area of radical politics, not yet on their own behalf, but, like the women of the thirties, on behalf of other causes. They were involved in the peace movement.

But more important for feminism, they were involved in the civil rights' movement.

And just as the fight in the 1840s and 1850s for the abolition of slavery had spurred women to fight for their own freedom, so the fight in the 1960s against racism spurred a renewed battle against sexism. Women, feeling oppressed themselves, identified with the blacks, and grew angry. And, for the first time in fifty years, they raised their voices and began to fight back.

But it was not just the civil rights' movement that spurred women to fight for their own rights. Once the technology of the nineteenth century had freed women through household machinery, and the birth-control devices of the twentieth century had allowed her to choose when she wanted to have a baby, the freedom of women was inevitable. It was simply a matter of time, and the time had come.

On August 26, 1970, thousands of women across the United States joined in parades, meetings, and demonstrations, to celebrate the fiftieth anniversary of the day women won the right to vote. Some of the slogans that day were funny: "Don't Cook Dinner—Starve a Rat Today!" and "Don't Iron While the Strike Is Hot!" But the aims of the National Women's Strike for Equality that day were serious. The women were demanding equality of jobs, pay, and education; free round-the-clock child-care centers; free abortions for all women who want abortions; and the passage of the Equal Rights Amendment to the Constitution.

On that day, there were so many demonstrations across the country, and the women's movement had obviously become so widespread, that politicians everywhere began to realize that they had better take the movement seriously. That day marked a turning point in the history of women; they had emerged from the cave into the sunlight and meant to stay there.

There are many organized groups of women all over the United States who are fighting for women's rights.

NOW—the National Organization of Women—was begun in 1965 by Betty Friedan. It continues to be the only woman's rights organization of its kind organized on a national level; it has chapters throughout the country. NOW members fight on both national and local levels against sex discrimination in employment, housing, and education; they fight for twenty-four-hour-universal-child-care; and also work to focus attention and gain support for the Equal Rights Amendment.

As NOW began to grow, other organizations began forming on a local level. Most were composed of women who were angry over job humiliations, who had suffered the horror of an illegal abortion, who were just plain miserable in their housewife roles. Many groups started simply as "rap" sessions designed to raise the consciousness of women socially and politically, to help them exchange views on their common troubles and problems. Many groups held demonstrations. In Atlantic City, they threw false eyelashes, padded bras, high-heeled shoes, and steno pads into a "freedom trash can" to demonstrate against the exploitation of women as represented by the Miss America pageant. (It was in Atlantic City that the myth of "bra-burners" began. In truth, feminists burned nothing at all.)

In New York City, feminists set up abortion referral services. In Boston, women picketed the Playboy Club. In Los Angeles, women broke into a CBS stockholders' meeting to protest the insulting image of women on the media. In Detroit, women dressed in black paraded past the city morgue to mourn dead sisters who were victims of illegal abortions.

All kinds of organizations have been springing up everywhere. Federally Employed Women (FEW) was founded in 1968 to fight discrimination in federal employment. The Women's Equity Action League (WEAL) was founded as an association of professional women to focus on legal action. Women journalists organized, and at the 1970 convention of the National Newspaper Guild, won support to end discrimination against women in press clubs and press boxes that had "male only" rules.

The National Association of Women Religious was organized in 1970 to protest their subservience to priests and bishops. There are also hundreds of women's caucuses and committees in individual businesses, in plants, in sports, in the media. Wherever there are women, women are talking about and fighting for equal rights. People are also recognizing the importance of the writings of women who are feminists or whose work makes comments on the nature of sexism: Virginia Woolf, Simone de Beauvoir, Doris Lessing, Anaïs Nin, Betty Friedan, Sylvia Plath, Kate Millet, Elaine Morgan, and many more.

The long silence is ended. In America, and with the growth of the movement in other countries, all over the world.

Section Three

WHAT YOU CAN DO ABOUT IT

Think Straight

A lot of people still think of Women's Liberation as a great, big, nasty machine invented to gobble up nice, little girls and sweet, devoted housewives and rearrange them somehow into mannish monsters who grow moustaches and eat barbed wire for breakfast.

The fact is that Women's Liberation is a very simple idea: a woman can be a woman without being treated like a slave, an inferior, a possession, or a child. A liberated woman is a woman who thinks of herself as a *human* being as well as a *sexual* being; who thinks of herself as an individual with her own interests and abilities, not as a sheep to be herded into whatever roles men choose for her. A liberated woman thinks of herself as as an equal, not a tag-along. Above all, a liberated woman is a woman who believes she has the same right to *choose* what she will do with her life as a man does and to take the same responsibility for her life as a man does.

To achieve this, we must come to think of all people as just that: people. The first step is to be *aware* of sexism, the division of people into male and female roles, in your own life experience.

Think about your early childhood. Were you given mostly dolls and dishes, while your brother or the boys in your neighborhood were given mostly cars, baseball bats, and building toys? In kindergarten, were the boys mostly encouraged to play with the cars and garages while you were plunked in front of the toy sink or icebox?

Were you brought up to think in terms of being pretty? Was your brother brought up to think in terms of being pretty?

Were you given as much freedom to run around the neighborhood as your brother or other boys? (Why not? Bad things can happen to little boys just as well as to little girls. We are made to feel afraid for our bodies much too young. By the same token, when we grow up, it's the boys who are sent into the army to fight, never the girls. Why? Does the world really think a girl's body is more precious than a boy's?)

When you were in elementary school, were the girls and boys treated the same way? (They probably didn't behave the same way. Your memory of those years is probably that the boys were noisy and got punished more often, and the girls were quieter and got better marks. That's mostly because girls and boys are brought up differently at home.) But did the teachers make any effort to even things out? Did they encourage the girls to be more aggressive? Did they encourage the boys to take pride in neatness or spelling marks? If you think back, the standards for girls and boys were different, weren't they?

And at home. What was it like at home? How old were you when you were given the feeling that marriage to the "right" man was the most, if not the only, important thing in a girl's life? (It's possible your mother hasn't mentioned *your* marriage yet, but how often do you hear her discuss other women's lives *only* in terms of their marriages? "Doris's life is awful because she's married to the wrong man." Should a marriage totally ruin a life? Or, "Nancy must be miserable, she's never married and has no children." Why? Some women *prefer* not to get married and have children; they have other satisfactions in their work, in their friends, in their own inner resources. A friend who is a librarian and another who is a business executive both say they get very tired of having people cluck at them sympathetically because they didn't marry. They both could have married. They simply didn't choose to!)

And did the parents you knew talk to little boys about love and marriage in the same way? Or did they feel that his personal development, his education, the beginning of his career should not be interrupted by too early a marriage.

And speaking of little boys, while they were deciding whether to be a shortstop, an astronaut, or a police chief, what were you deciding to be? If it was more than somebody's mother or somebody's wife, was it a typically feminine, motherly career like teaching or nursing? Did it ever occur to you—or did anybody ever suggest to you—that you could be a woman jockey like Kathy Kusner, who was the first; that, like Linda Little of Oklahoma, you could climb telephone poles as a linewoman, instead of being an operator; that there are no women pilots on major American airlines (United Airlines states openly that "pilots must be of the male species"), and that you might be the first. The point is, were you brought up as boys are to seriously believe that you could be anything you wanted to be from a stunt rider to a nuclear physicist. Or was it planted somewhere in the back of your mind by your parents, your teachers, counselors, or friends that in this world there are boy careers and girl careers, men's work and women's work, and that they are separate or different in kind.

Were you a "ladylike" little girl? And if you weren't, were you called a "tomboy"—a way of saying "a girl doesn't need to explore and exercise her mind and muscles, but don't worry, she'll get over it and settle down nicely." (Why should an active girl be called an imitation boy?) Or were you allowed to be as active and curious and get your knees as dirty and scraped as the boys.

And if you fell down and cried, what then? Were you held and comforted? Were the boys? Or were they told to hold back their emotions while you were allowed to express yours. (The boys get the short end of it on this one! Men suffer a great deal because they are told to bottle up their emotions.)

Think about the differences now, in your teens. There must be hundreds of examples in your daily life that mark the separation of boys and girls into sex roles, that forbid girls to grow into equally mature and independent human beings.

In your school, is there a tracking system in which girls are given different courses from boys? In some schools, the system is really extreme, with the girls taking cooking and sewing classes; and boys taking machine shop, printing, mechanical drawing, and other classes that lead to useful work in the outside world. (Not that kitchen duty isn't useful, but everybody, not just girls, should learn how to feed hungry faces.) In other schools, there may not be such a division. But if there's no division of boys and girls in your school, is there a general feeling that boys do better in math and science and girls do better in the liberal arts? Are your career plans and work taken just as seriously as the boys'? Or is it assumed that it is more important for the boys to know how to make a living than the girls. And if you are being encouraged to work, are you being encouraged to make a serious commitment to the kind of work you want to do for the rest of your life? Or are you being taught to think just in terms of a temporary job, "just something to tide you over until you get married."

And what about the books you read? Are they always about

famous men? Have you ever been taught about famous women? I mean besides Betsy Ross (sewing), Florence Nightingale (nursing), and Queen Victoria (who had lots of babies and adored Prince Albert). Surely the history of the suffragists and the struggle for women's rights is as important as the history of all those men on horses in the Middle Ages. And after all, Jane Austen's novels are just as good as Charles Dickens's, and Mary Wollstonecraft's political writings just as important as any written by men.

It's a real put-down to be taught over and over again how great men are—and never to hear anything about the great work women have done.

Think about the attitudes of the girls and boys you know. Do the boys talk mostly about sports, their careers, what's going on in the world, about cars and machines, about sex and politics and the army—while girls talk mostly about boys, love and marriage, clothes and silver patterns? Do the boys think in terms of themselves, while the girls think in terms of the boys? Why isn't everybody concerned equally about all these things?

Learning to be aware of sexism wherever you find it, wherever you see it, hear it, or experience it, is the first step toward freedom. In books, in school texts or novels, on television, in movies, in magazines, in the attitudes of your friends, your parents, teachers, advisors, the boys you date, you'll begin to react whenever girls are spoken of or treated as helpless, childish idiots.

After you've learned to scream instead of laugh every time Archie Bunker calls Edith a "dingbat"—or, more generally speaking, after you've learned to be aware that society is not very fair to girls—think about whether you are always fair to yourself and other girls you know. Girls often betray themselves without knowing it—by siding with boys against other girls, by joining in laughter at jokes against women, by secretly feeling males are more important.

The brain has no sex. Do you truly understand and believe that boys are not born with better minds than girls? Or do you still feel instinctively that boys have "different" minds or "better" minds.

"Feminine" and "masculine" are just words that describe sex, like "male" and "female." Do you really feel somewhere inside you that there are basic feminine personality traits like self-sacrifice and submission and basic masculine traits like aggression and strength? Or do you understand that it's not males and females who are born different, but all people who are born different. People have been brainwashed into thinking there are inborn differences between boys and girls, when those differences are really a matter of training and of individual differences in people that occur regardless of sex. (An example is the widespread belief that women are born with better instincts for the care of children than men. There are too many wonderful male counselors, male teachers, male pediatricians, male social workers, to say nothing of the growing number of superb and caring fathers, to support such a belief any longer. The reason more mothers than fathers take over child care is simply that they have been told it is their function in life to do so.)

Make a list of all the traits you consider masculine, and all the traits you consider feminine. Do all the boys and girls you know fit neatly into those categories? If not, do you consider them peculiar? If a girl you knew wanted to be an architect, and a boy you knew wanted to be a nursery school teacher, would you think of the girl as "masculine" and the boy as "feminine"? Is there something wrong with a boy who loves cooking or a girl who loves racing cars? Or do you really believe that we are all human beings with the individual right to love, hate, and work at whatever we wish?

What about your own plans? How do you feel about the traditional sex-role system? Do you take your work in school seriously? Do you plan a career? Do you think marriage is every girl's solution to life? If you're planning to marry someday, do you think the housework and the care of the children should be shared? Or is all that a woman's responsibility. If you marry, will you go on working? Will your husband's interests always come before yours? Do you think you would be a failure if you didn't marry and have children? Do you think you would be a failure if you didn't have a career? Do you think you will need a man to "take care of" you? Or will you be able to take care of yourself and love a man as a free and independent person?

If you are absolutely truthful with yourself, you may find some of your own answers surprising. You may be freer than you thought, or not so free after all. A lot of people are more prejudiced against themselves than they think, and the way you think of yourself becomes, after a while, the way other people think of you.

What about Boys?

Girls in junior high schools and high schools across the country have begun to get together and talk about the feelings and problems they have as girls, examining themselves in the light of the women's movement. In one discussion group held at a medium-sized junior high school in a large city, these were some of the answers to questions I asked.

Madeleine: "I think the biggest problem girls have is boys. If you don't have a boyfriend, everybody thinks you're a failure. And if you do have a boyfriend, you have to change your whole personality around to keep him."

Margot: "If you have a different opinion, you don't dare argue back too much. Boys don't like girls to be brainy. But the bad part is, after you act dumb to please them, they think you really are dumb. It makes me sick."

Pam: "What I hate is the list of rules and regulations about what a boy is supposed to do and what a girl is supposed to do. For instance, if a girl is feminine she's supposed to get the boy to do certain things for her, like carry her books. I once saw a boy with his arms full of books, his books and *her* books, try-ing to get a door open besides—while she just stood there wait-ing and doing nothing. It looked pretty funny."

Deirdre: "What bothers me is not being able to call a boy up if you like him and want to have a date. I grew up with a boy who was a very good friend. When we were younger, I could just call him up and say 'come on over.' When you're in your teens, you can't do that anymore. You can't just be friends. And if you call a boy for a date, everybody says you're chasing him."

Margot: "If you like a boy, all you can do is flirt and wear sexy clothes and wait by the telephone. If you make one real move in his direction, you're called aggressive."

Liz: "The boy I go out with never has any money. He gets a very small allowance. I get a bigger allowance, and I'd be happy to pay for our dates. But he says it makes him feel bad if a girl pays, so we end up doing nothing. I don't see why it has to be that way, with the boy paying all the time."

Madeleine: "Once I liked a guy a lot, and he didn't call. After about three weeks, my mother suggested I give a party and use that as an excuse to call him up. I did it, but I really didn't like having to play games like that. My mother said I better get used to it. You have to play games to get the boy you want. Even after you're married, the woman has to play games to get the man to do what she wants."

Margot: "I get so tired of worrying all the time whether I'm pretty and sexy enough. I remember when I went to my first dance in the seventh grade. All I did for days ahead of time was worry about whether some boy would ask me to dance or whether I'd be a wallflower. I wonder how the boys would like it if they had to spend half their lives worrying about whether they were handsome and sexy or if some girl was going to ask them to dance."

Liz: "Another problem with the boys paying for everything all the time is I always feel sort of as if they had bought me for the evening, so I have to do what they want and go where they want. If they do ask you, it makes you feel uncomfortable because you never know how much money they have. Sometimes I'll want an extra hamburger or I'll want to take a taxi instead of a bus, but you can't really ask them if they have enough money. I don't see why girls can't pay for things as well as boys. It would solve a lot of problems."

Pam: "One problem it would solve is the feeling you get when a boy has taken you out and spent money on you that you owe him a kiss goodnight. If each of you paid half or you took turns paying, you wouldn't have to feel you owed him anything. Last week I went out with a boy who took me to a movie and then out for a hamburger. When he took me home, he said he had spent all his money on me and didn't I think he deserved at least something for it. It made me feel like a prostitute."

Madeleine: "Aside from the money, there's always that thing about if you don't make out with them, will they ask you out again."

Margot: "In school, a lot of girls won't enter discussions or come out with answers to questions because they think it's unfeminine to sound too smart. Girls are always putting down their own intelligence in front of boys. And girls act silly and giggle when boys are around in a way they wouldn't do if they were just with other girls. I know, because I do it myself sometimes. It's degrading when you think about it afterward."

Pam: "For a long time, the boys in our class were calling all the girls 'dingbats.' I wish television didn't have such a bad image of women. Women are always in the kitchen or taking care of the kids and waiting for the man to come home from work. Or else they have emotional problems some man has to solve for them. Like 'Marcus Welby.' It's about two doctors who take care of everybody, usually a girl who's in trouble. Why can't they have a program about a woman doctor who takes care of people's problems?"

Liz: "It's not just television, it's everywhere. In the movies, it's always the woman who's the sexy one, while the man catches the criminals or whatever. Or else she's the one who sacrifices everything. Like *Love Story.* The boy goes on to law school, but she has to give up her music to support him. And in the teen magazines, it's always the feminine girl who gets the boy. Or if you look at *Vogue,* you can really get an inferiority complex. You not only have to be feminine, you have to be thin and fantastically gorgeous besides. Everywhere you look, you see something that emphasizes sex roles. The boys have to be successful and rich, the girls have to be beautiful and meek."

Margot: "I think our worst problem is all we ever talk about or think about is boys. Listen to us right now! The way the boys behave is a big problem. But the biggest problem is ourselves. We're the ones who have to change. We have to think of ourselves as people who need to be fulfilled as human beings. We have to want to be somebody on our own, not just part of the life of some boy. And anyway, who says we have to get married at all! My aunt never married, and she's perfectly happy. She says she likes her privacy and coming and going when she pleases instead of when everyone else pleases. I know one thing; I'm not going to get married unless I want to. I'm not going to get married just because society says I should."

Deirdre: "I want to be a biologist. I want to have a family, too. I just couldn't spend my life housekeeping the way my mother does. Even she agrees you get the feeling your whole life has been wasted if being a housewife is all you do. But when I tell a boy I want to do both, he usually says I won't have time to do both, that if the wife works, who takes care of things at home"?

Margot: "Would you really marry a man who felt that way? My mother is a pediatrician. She's always worked and she's always been a mother, too. She says men who still think a woman's place is in the home are prehistoric! I agree with what the women's liberation movement says, that both women and men should be able to do the work they want to do and that they should both have the fun of bringing up their children together. I think in a lot of families the men work so hard they never have time for their children. And if all the woman does is take care of her children, she gets too emotionally tied to them. If a woman works and shares the expenses, and a man shares bringing up the children, it gives everybody a chance to be a person on his own and part of the family, too."

Liz: "I know a boy who once admitted to me that he was scared of having to be responsible for a wife and children, like what if he couldn't get a job or something. Maybe the sex-role system isn't fair to men either, making them responsible for earning all the money. I think maybe the boys get tired of having to be big and tough all the time, just the way we get tired of having to be pretty and feminine."

Pam: "A boy said to me once, 'I get tired of always being the one who has to make the phone call. One day I was feeling bad, and it would have been nice if the girl I was dating had called me for a change.' "

Madeleine: "I really do want to be a housewife. I want to stay home and take care of my children when they're young. What I like about women's liberation is when they say it's okay to be a housewife, and you shouldn't let anybody put it down. I mean, it's a job that should be considered just as important a job as a man's job, and people shouldn't laugh at it. They shouldn't laugh at a man either, if he wants to stay home and take care of the kids while his wife works."

Deirdre: "There's a boy in our class who doesn't fit the

strong-arm male stereotype at all. He's quiet and gentle. He says his parents keep pushing him to get on the football team. What happens when he grows up? Does he have to go get himself killed in a war in order to prove he's a man?"

By the time the discussion was over, the girls had agreed on a number of points. Their first agreement was that girls should be equal with boys. And since this was so, they felt that girls should call boys to go out as well as the other way around, that girls should pay for dates as well as boys. That way, decisions about where to go and what to do would be shared, and the girl would not feel she had been "rented" for the evening. Even more important, the girl would not feel she had to pay back for the evening sexually. This system would give girls more self-respect, and with more self-respect they might not worry so much about pleasing a boy by playing dumb and pretty to make sure he called back.

The girls felt that their biggest problem was not necessarily the boys' reaction to this, but the reactions of their parents, some of whom had very traditional ideas about dating, and about male and female roles. They thought it would be helpful to try to explain their views to their parents.

Madeleine: "It isn't easy to change things. But I think if our parents and teachers will try to understand and help, things can change. Like at home, our mothers getting the boys to help with the laundry instead of always us. Or at dances, making sure the girls have a chance to ask the boys to dance as well as the other way around. We've got to turn the older generation on as well as ourselves."

I wished them well with all my heart!

What about Work?

Do you ever talk to other girls and women who are turned on to the women's liberation movement about what kind of person you want to be, about what kind of work you want to do?

Girls and women all over the country are discovering that it's only by getting together with other women that we'll ever find out who we are and what kind of people we want to be. It's no longer possible to accept male value judgments about a woman's role. We have accepted their value judgments too long. We have trusted men to think things out, not each other. There is a sisterhood among women now. We are at last learning to trust each other.

Rap groups (consciousness-raising sessions) are the basic

units of the women's movement and are springing up every-where: in high schools, on college and university campuses, among young girls and mature women who have found them-selves trapped in female roles in their marriages or in their jobs. A man once asked me why it was necessary to organize rap groups. The explanation is that while men always had someplace to get together everyday and be themselves—at the office, in bars, in sport groups, in clubs—women were isolated in their houses, isolated from each other. Even young girls are often isolated, because when they are together they tend to be competitive over boys rather than supportive of each other. When I said this at a high school meeting once, a teenage girl burst into tears and answered, "I always thought there must be something wrong with me because I felt alone. I didn't realize other girls felt they had no one to talk to."

There is somebody else who understands. The girl sitting next to you in class, the woman sitting next to you on the bus or the subway, the saleswoman in the store, a woman teacher at school, and, believe it or not, your mother. They may not agree with you, they may be on the defensive about women's liberation (if they have not been free themselves), but they understand. They know what it means to be a woman.

Do you, when you think about the kind of work you want to do, let yourself consider all the fields that should be avail-able? Do you believe you can do what you want to do? If the problem is job opportunity, there are legal ways to fight back, and women's groups all over the country to help support you in your fight for the job you want. If there isn't a group in your particular town or company, you can start one. For advice about sex discrimination at school or at work, for advice on how to set up women's groups (and girls' groups!) to fight for or discuss or cope with the problems in any area of women's rights, here is a list of groups you can write to. They will an-swer your letters and will refer you to a local chapter for guidance.

Women's Action Alliance, 370 Lexington Avenue, New York, N.Y. 10017. This is a national, nonprofit women's group which is organizing an information and referral system on women's activities.

High School Student Information Center, 1010 Wisconsin Avenue, N.W. Washington, D.C. 20007. They will send you information on how to organize girls' groups in school and offer guidance on how to cope with sex discrimination.

National Organization for Women, 1957 East 73rd Street, Chicago, Illinois 60649. NOW has national task forces working on every area of discrimination against women. Write for local chapter addresses.

I mention these organizations here, because the likelihood of your getting good guidance at school is problematical. As you know, it's one thing to decide on a job or a career and another to find the proper guidance and the opportunity to go through with it. Girls have always suffered from lack of support!

Besides the lack of good advice and good support, there is something else many girls lack because of early conditioning— self-esteem. Girls suffer from a lack of faith in themselves and in each other. *Trans-Action* magazine reported experiments several years ago showing that when the same lecture was given by a female teacher and a male teacher, women college students rated the male "better." When a group of high-school students were asked whether they would vote for a woman president, many of them answered that they felt a man could do a "better" job. When I met with a group of black female high-school students who were involved with the black movement at their school, most of the girls agreed that the boys knew more about politics. One girl said, however, "I get so sick of going out for Cokes and sandwiches, typing letters, and running the mimeograph machine. In spite of Angela Davis, the guys say it's up to them to do the thinking, and up to us to help them by running the machines. What I say is, it's hard enough to be put down because I'm black without being put down because I'm a woman, too. No point in having liberation for half a race."

Most working girls and women, even young ones, have permitted their roles to be defined by everyone but themselves. (People—mostly men, but not always—are forever saying things like "women are happier serving men," "women are happier when men take charge," "women are happier when someone else does the thinking for them." Among many women, phrases like that cause a terrible grinding of the teeth!) Most women are aware that they are just as capable as the men they work with, sometimes even more capable. But they simply do not reach for the rewards their capacities entitle them to or even for ordinary equality. A woman I met who has worked for the same company for ten years knows how the firm should be run better than anyone else. She has trained a dozen or more young men to fill the position just above her own. It's idiotic! I asked her why she didn't request the job herself. Her answer was a slight shrug, half a smile, and the words, "What do you expect? I'm only a woman."

The women I know who have "made it" are generally those who expect to be treated as an equal. Sometimes, of course, they don't get as far as men with the same capacity, without trying harder and fighting for what they want. But if they've done it, so can the rest of us. Remember, there are women now in almost every field, not just the professions and the sciences. Even the crafts that require apprenticeship training and were once traditionally closed to women, the machinists, electricians, and carpenters, now admit women. In 1969 there were about 1,800 women learning to be laboratory technicians, plumbers, aircraft and auto mechanics, shoemakers, construction workers, watchmakers, and skilled workers of other kinds. They are earning twice or more the salaries they would have earned as secretaries. So when you're thinking about the kind of work you want to do, remember—there isn't anything you can't do as well as a man and maybe better! (I mention these crafts and skills especially in answer to the protest I've sometimes heard that the women's movement seems to be geared toward those women who want to be doctors, lawyers, or astrophysicists. One girl wailed at me not long ago, "I've never gotten a mark higher than C in my life. All I'm fit for is to be somebody's stenographer." As it turned out, she happened to be pretty good with her hands, and when I mentioned carpentry among other possibilities, her face lit up. It just hadn't occurred to her that women were "allowed" that kind of trade.)

All of which is to say that the myths about women who work are being exploded: the myth that women are not creative; the idea that women in government, in industry, and offices should have the jobs that are closest to housekeeping and a wife's duties; the myth that women actually prefer helping a *man* "do his thing" and only want to feel needed; and the myth that any woman who does big jobs, thinks for herself, and is successful must either be a nasty bitch or be sleeping with the man who helped her to the top. These are ridiculous man-made myths. Up until now most people have accepted them, however, as truth—which is why so many women have accepted low-paying jobs and dead-end positions. That these myths have lasted so long is due to prejudice on the part of men and low self-esteem on the part of women.

Low self-esteem also accounts for all the volunteer work women do. Giving *some* time for the good of the community is something all people should do, men as well as women. But the middle-class housewife who does no paid work and devotes all of her time to volunteer activities does so because she has the secret feeling that, though she wants to work, she isn't worth much. Volunteer work gives women the feeling they are needed, but not that their work has a *value*. Just as women in families fall into the trap of supporting and encouraging everybody's needs but their own, just as women go into the "helping" professions, just as the feminists of the past ended up fighting for everybody's right but their own, women also go into the community to help everybody but themselves. Women have been saddled with being the tender and compassionate members of society whose primary purpose is to answer the telephone whenever anyone else puts in an emotional call. We answer the call because we have been trained to enjoy feeling "needed." But the time has come to let the other half of the human race share the pleasure of being *needed*, while we share the pleasure of being *valued* and *paid!* (If you want to go into a service vocation, by all means plan to do so, but get a degree or at least some training—you'll be worth a lot more to society and you'll find your work a lot more satisfying, if you know what you're doing.)

There is another pitfall girls sometimes encounter when they begin to plan their lives and careers, and that is deciding to do the kind of work you can do at home. The picture of the happy housewife painting, sculpting, or writing away with the children climbing around her knees is a pleasant picture—but a nearly impossible one. Creative work requires privacy. It takes a great deal of discipline for a man or a woman to work at home. But if a man works at home, his wife keeps the kids strictly out of his way. Unless you are rich enough to have a housekeeper or sensible enough to find a husband who is willing to take over for several hours a day, or unless you plan not to have children at all—be aware that young children and work at home do not mix well. A nine-to-five job, with a clear-cut barrier between professional work and housework, requires much less discipline. By working at home, a woman risks turning into the family ogre by screaming for time and privacy; she risks losing her sanity from the constant interruptions of household affairs; and she risks getting so little done that she ends up earning very little or letting her career slip away entirely. (When my children were babies, I risked those things daily. I made it though because I have a husband who took over for a few hours each day and stood faithful guard at my door. A close friend of mine who is a painter was less fortunate. Her husband traveled a good deal on business. She finally had to rent studio space away from her home in order to get any work done at all.)

More than ever before, women are breaking through the work barriers set up by men, women are learning to esteem themselves more highly, women are earning higher salaries. This is because women have at last learned to talk to each other, to discuss their common problems, to compare their solutions, to stand together and fight together for their lives.

It's hard to go it alone. But if you are a person who respects herself as someone with the right to be fully human, and if you are brave (and you will need to be brave, because there are still a lot of people around to hassle you for not getting a thrill out of the idea of being a household slave), understand that there are a lot of us around now. If you need help, holler.

What about Marriage?

Marriage can begin in a lot of different ways at many different stages of a person's life. Just as boys are prodded early to think in terms of making a living, girls are prodded to think in terms of making a nest. It is rarely suggested to a girl that she need not marry, that marriage is just one of the possible choices. Mostly, girls are convinced, and convinced young, that in marriage lies the most important part of their future. Here are a few samples of the ways in which these marriages may happen:

Sample Marriage Number One begins in the sixth grade. She has been brought up in a household where everybody keeps strictly to traditional sex roles. Under her mother's eye, she has learned how to cook, sew on her brother's buttons, launder her father's socks (cute, wifely little thing, isn't she?), and stay clean and out of trouble (the kind of trouble caused by being curious enough about something to want to take it apart, to run somewhere different and explore it, to climb on it, jump over it, or make a mess with it). She has learned how to get what she wants by flattering men, not earning things herself. She has learned to be "adorable" not direct. She has learned that it isn't necessary to "bother her pretty little head" with thinking, because men will always do that for her. She has understood that while it's true women do all the dirty work, there are two rewards for that: the first is that she will always be taken care of; the second is that she can have the fun of being a martyr. She has learned that the man is the center of all creation, certainly the magic center of a woman's life, and that without one, a woman is nothing. She has been told to pay no attention to the workings of politics, industry, the arts, sciences, or the rest of the great big world out there (clearly men's business), because the greatest act of creativity is having a baby (her business). She may even be taught to feel that this makes her better than a man. It's the "hand-that-rocks-the-cradle-and-winds-a-man-around-her-finger" syndrome (an untrue myth told by men and repeated by mother to daughter to make women happy believing they have a power that they, in fact, do not have at all). She grows up believing, however, that her only way to power and status is by serving a man, by making him dependent on her. He will take care of her, and she will share his status and his glory.

With all this in mind, she has been playing house since the day she was first able to hold a doll. "You be the daddy, I'll be the mommy," has always been her favorite game.

She plays the game for real the minute she can get a boy to respond. This can be as early as the sixth grade. She singles out the boy who seems most willing to be flattered by her adoration and clamps on tight. She will follow him anywhere, do whatever he wishes. And because she has been trained so early in the feminine arts, she will keep his attention. She may have to try two or three boys in the beginning, but she will find one early in her life, keep him, and marry him. She will have to. Her entire life and self-esteem depends on it.

Her future? She will go on following him anywhere. Anywhere his company moves him, she will uproot her life and follow him, leaving friends, home, subordinating everything to his interests, his career. She will live in constant anxiety over whether he still loves her—she will diet, buy face creams, and spend hours in beauty parlors. Having no life experience or thoughts of her own, she will know, as they get older, that she bores him. She can turn to her children for comfort, but they will grow up and leave home. Her nest is empty, her marriage is empty, she is empty. There is nothing left but her martyrdom and her kitchen floor, both of which she shined up yesterday, shined up today, and will shine up tomorrow.

Sample Marriage Number Two begins during the middle of the teenage years. She believes in love, in romantic love. She, too, has been brought up in a house where everybody lives according to traditional sex roles. Only in this case, her parents' marriage is actively unhappy. Instead of exploring why an unequal marriage leads to frustration, her mother explains the bad marriage simply by saying she married the wrong man. Her mother often talks about past men in her life and wonders how it would have been if she had married differently. This one would have earned more money; that one would have had a more important position; another would have led a more glamorous life. It never occurs to the mother to teach her daughter to earn some of those things for herself—all comes through a man, the right man. In return for what the man does, a girl must be pretty, sexy, and charming at all times. The daughter is taught to be bewitching early in her teens, and she gets approval, not for work she has done well, but for the ex-

tent of her popularity with boys. Because of her parents' unhappy marriage and the constant misery at home, the girl's one
idea is to escape and escape fast. She has not been taught to
work or to earn her own way; she *has* been taught that True
Love with Mr. Right is the only answer to her happiness. So
the obvious solution is to fall in love and get married—quick!
Which she does.

Because she believes in Romance and has no true concep-
tion of what adult love means—interests in common, mutual
respect, wanting the same things out of life, the excitement of
knowing another person really well—her marriage gets stale
in a very short time. After all, it's not very *romantic* to clean
house while your husband works and then comes home tired.
She may take a job (it won't be an interesting one because she
hasn't been trained to do much) or decide to have children
(which is one of life's great joys but hardly romantic). In either case, she finds out after a few years that her world is no
longer the picture of True Love she had envisioned. Like her
mother before her, she does not understand that a woman has
to fill her own emptiness herself, that no man can do it for her.
Instead, as her mother did, she will blame her unhappiness on
her choice of husband. She has three ways to go from there to
recapture the romance and the fun she misses: she can take a
lover; she can get a divorce and try again; or she can make a
career out of her misery as her mother did.

Sample Marriage Number Three begins in the late teens
after high school. She has been encouraged to use her mind
some. Her mother may work now, or may have worked in the
past, not because she enjoyed it, but to "help out" with the
family budget. She has been told that she will have to "help
out" with a job until she gets married, and that she may even
have to "help out" with a job if her husband doesn't earn much
after she gets married. But she will not be allowed to think
that any work she can do will be really worthwhile or that she

can earn very much. Work in this case is not meant to fill her with pride or result from special interests or give her a feeling of accomplishment and independence. Most likely she will take any job she can get and quit with a sigh of relief the minute she finds someone to marry or at least as soon as the man can support her. "Whoever earns the money" in her life will always be the one whose decisions must be respected. If she stays home to care for the house, the children, the garden, the finances, the cooking, the laundry, and works a seven-to-ten-o'clock schedule, this still won't make her equal with her husband in her own eyes because she isn't earning a salary for the work. Because she has worked and has acquired a little of the sense of self-reliance earning money gives you, she will respect this in her husband and lose respect for herself. On the other hand, the work she did was dull, she had no personal ambition to seek promotion, and she will use "who'll take care of the children?" and, after they've gone to school, "who'll take care of the house?" as excuses not to go back to a boring job, unless money is desperately needed. In guilty return for the fact that her husband faces what she believes to be the boring work of the world every day of his life, she will bring him his pipe and slippers to the day he stops drawing breath. Money should never equal power in a family, but for her it always will.

Sample Marriage Number Four begins in college or shortly thereafter. She comes from a family where education is given great importance, where girls are encouraged to do as well in school as boys. In her teens her parents applaud her good marks far more than the number of dates she has. At home she hears her father respectfully listen to her mother's opinions and sees him help out with the dishes and other housework. Because her parents respect each other too much to discuss problems in front of the children, their daughter may never inquire too closely into the workings of the marriage. (For instance, the fact that the father helps out with *her* dishes, *her* laundry, *her* kitchen floor, takes out *her* garbage—why isn't it *their* dishes, *their* laundry, *their* kitchen floor, *their* garbage!) Her mother may have a career, but it is clearly also her mother's responsibility to run the house. Nobody questions the fact that the mother has to assume two sets of responsibilities, career and marriage, while the father is really responsible—despite his help with the house and child care—only for his own career.

So although the girl is brought up to take her schoolwork seriously and to think in terms of an interesting career, she is still given to understand that in marriage, the man's work comes first. She is given to understand something else, too, although it is very little mentioned during her growing years. She is *without question expected to get married* as a first priority. This becomes apparent when she sets out for college, at which time she discovers from her parents that she has been sent only partly to get an education and only partly to prepare for a career. Mostly she has been sent to college to find a really first-class husband; her own education will fit her out to be the kind of wife an educated and successful man needs. The emphasis has suddenly shifted from her becoming a fully developed and independent person to becoming a first-rate wife.

It is girls like this one, the ones who have been educated to use their minds and their abilities and who then have to sink to second place in the household career scene—or very often have to give up their work entirely if their husbands' companies uproot them or if they live a "company" or "suburban" life that requires a lot of entertaining or playing "lady" at luncheons or in volunteer groups to advance their husbands' careers—who end up as alcoholics, on pills, or in psychotherapy. The frustration of giving up the pursuits of a well-educated mind, or the guilt and anxiety produced by having a career and also being totally responsible for the home (you generally get the feeling you're not doing either as well as you should) can be very difficult to bear. (It's still better, however, to bear both responsibilities if necessary than to have no career at all—if the anxiety rate is higher, there is also much pleasure and pride to make up for it.) There is no more frustrated person in the world than an educated woman who exchanges a major in philosophy for diapers. (This is why male chauvinists will say, "It's a mistake to educate women at all.") The answer obviously is not less training of the mind, but more training in self-esteem.

Sample Marriage Number Five begins at any age with any girl who does not think of herself first and foremost as someone who has to get married to be a person. She thinks of herself as a full human being, free to make any and all choices. She will make the best use of her education and training. She will take her pick of any field or career that interests her and suits her talents. If she finds doors closed to her, she will not accept the fact meekly. She will bang the doors open, not by wearing a tighter sweater, but by using her mind, her will, her own strength and the organized strength of her sisters in a direct and open way as befits dignified people.

What is important to her in her relationship with a man is not the status an engagement ring is supposed to give, but a relationship that is founded on equality. When she marries, they will both work, they will both share the housework of *their* household. If there are to be children (and there is no reason in the world why just because they *can* have children they *must* have them—in this overpopulated world there are no sociological or economic reasons arguing for the necessity of children) they will share the responsibility for bringing them up. They will not believe the myth that just because a woman carries a child she is best suited to nurture it. They will believe, instead, that both men and women can be nurturing and supportive and that both men and women can be aggressive and independent. They do not believe that it is the man's responsibility alone to support the family any more than they believe it is the woman's responsibility to do all the cooking. If she needs more education, he will work. If he needs more education, she will work. They may both work part time, tend house and children part time. If a move becomes necessary to either career, both careers will be given equal weight in the discussion regardless of who is earning more money. They will live together as two free and independent human beings who *choose* to share their lives—not as "feminine" and "masculine" types shackled together for society's approval. In freeing herself to be what she needs to be, she knows she is freeing him as well to live as he wants to live. She will not expect him to be a big, strong man twenty-four hours a day, nor will he think of her as his darling nincompoop. They will both be strong when necessary, and both will have the right to lean a little when necessary. A girl may even elect to follow the traditional housewife-mother role, but she knows that she does it of her own free choice and knows that eventually men will also be free to elect the househusband-father role if they choose. No marriage is ever guaranteed. But an equal marriage, a liberated marriage stands the best chance of making both partners happy.

Certainly you do not have to decide as a teenager whether you do or do not want to get married. But it isn't too early to think about how you regard yourself as a person and how you relate to the boys you date. If you consider the kinds of marriages discussed in this chapter, you may find some traits you recognize in yourself, your friends, your parents. You may find you want to change some of the patterns you've been following, or you may be satisfied right now with the way you feel.

The most important thing is to understand that you are as free to choose what you will do with your life as any boy in your class and that you are entitled to exactly the same right to fulfill your needs as he is. That is the whole point of women's liberation.

The Fight for
Your Own Survival

I have heard many girls and women say that coming upon the
ideas of the women's movement is like walking out of a small,
dark room into the sun. To realize that other women feel con-
stricted by the roles normally given to women, to know that
women everywhere are at last demanding to choose their des-
tinies instead of being handed the limiting roles of sex object,
goddess (not much room to move on top of a pedestal),
mother, wife, dependent servant, to understand that it's not
just you, but all women, who are tired of feeling that it's a
handicap to be born female—to be aware of these things brings
an incredible measure of relief.

Liberation is based first on personal choices. It begins with the knowledge that you need never take second place to a man. It means that you do not have to choose between femininity and achievement—you can have both. It means that you can choose marriage, children, and a career (as men always have), instead of having to give up one part of your life for another. It means that you need not marry and have children at all, or if you do, that you can marry a man who believes in equal sharing or that you can make use of day-care centers (or co-operative baby-sitting arrangements) for your children. Liberation is knowing you have the right to be a housewife, an astronaut, or both, and that you will fight for that right if necessary.

Liberation is also a willingness to fight publicly for what you believe. You won't get far by having the secret feeling you're an equal human being—and then not answering a question in class because the boys might not approve of an intelligent girl. Nor will it help you much to know you can do a job perfectly well and then to take less money for it than they would pay a man. There's not much point in getting annoyed over women being treated as sex objects, and then using a good pair of legs to get yourself a job, or a promotion, or a raise. It won't help you to grumble about being tracked into sewing, cooking, and home-economics classes in school unless you're willing to struggle with the administration to change the tracking system so that both boys and girls can take cooking and/or machine shop. In social situations, you can't really believe in yourself as a girl if you laugh at or pass off anti-women jokes and remarks. This doesn't mean you shouldn't have a sense of humor, but truly derogatory remarks are seldom really funny. When you betray yourself in any of these ways, you are also betraying other girls and women. And conversely, when you win in any given situation, you've won not only for yourself, but for the next girl who comes along.

Groups of women are fighting many public battles today— for equal pay and job opportunities, for the right of every woman to decide whether she wants to continue a pregnancy or not, for the right to equal education, for fairer property and divorce laws, for an end to the ridiculous and demeaning image of women in movies, advertisements, television, and books, for federal funds for child-care centers, to elect both male and female legislators who will promote the cause of women's rights, and above all, to put an end to thousands of years of discrimination against women politically, legally, and culturally. Women everywhere are working to reeducate the public by appearing on television and radio, by holding conferences, by writing books, by demonstrating and picketing. And to an even greater extent they are doing it by long conversations everywhere they go—in laundromats and supermarkets, over cups of coffee and the heads of their playing children, in luncheonettes and offices, in factories, in schools— wherever two or more women get together these days, they talk.

The most important people women can talk to are their daughters. I had a rare and touching experience one night not long ago. For months, I had been ranting and raving at every television commercial, every movie, every antifeminist remark that escaped unwittingly from my son or my husband (men, however decent, can't be changed overnight), and discussing the chapters of this book with my family as I wrote them. Not a newspaper article, an unfair job situation that came to my attention, an action taken by the women's movement, escaped my comment. The household had had quite a dose of women's liberation. But since my daughter is young, I had no real notion about how much of it was affecting her. That truly, in the deepest part of her, she understood, I saw during a game of charades. She pointed upward for the first part of the word in a movie title, and as our guess was incorrect, she began on the second part of the word. She made a rocking motion with her arms, as if to rock a baby. My son and I guessed words like mother, nurse, grandmother, nanny, while my daughter grew more and more impatient and puzzled. She didn't change her motion, but went on rocking harder than ever. Several times in a row she went over the title, first pointing upward, then making the rocking-the-baby motion. Finally, we gave up, and she said, "Oh for goodness sake, it was so easy. *The Godfather* is the answer. You were so busy thinking of mothers every time I rocked the baby, that's why you didn't get it. Why couldn't you think of fathers rocking a baby?"

Why, indeed! We older ones have to be trained to think what, thank heaven, comes perfectly naturally to her. Feminism may not have reached every corner of my mind yet, but my daughter is part of a whole new generation who, I hope, will have no truck with stereotyped sex roles, who will not think of "men's work" and "women's work," of man as the provider and woman as the childbearer, of man as the strong, responsible one and woman as the one who needs to be taken care of. My daughter and all of you can make different choices from the ones your mothers and I made. But what we are all learning, all the generations together, is that it is a wonderful thing to be a woman, a strong, independent, able woman who is free to stretch and stretch and stretch until she can admire herself because of her own efforts rather than seek admiration in the eyes of a boy or a man.

Never mind the jeers of those who are quick to remind us of what we have not yet done. Who knows what women will accomplish when they have learned finally to be free? Who knows what the intelligence of women will contribute to the world now that the search of women for themselves has finally begun?

Suggested Reading

Bird, Caroline. *Born Female*. New York: Pocket Books, 1969 (paperback)—describes the kind of job discrimination women face.

De Beauvoir, Simone. *The Second Sex*. New York: Bantam, 1968 (paperback)—an explanation of the historical status of women as the opposite of man, through mythology, history, literature, biology. Difficult but fascinating reading.

Firestone, Shulamith. *The Dialectic of Sex*. New York: Morrow, 1970—radical feminism by a leading member of the women's movement.

Friedan, Betty. *The Feminine Mystique*. New York: Dell, 1964 (paperback)—mind-opening study of the exploitation of women who have given up careers to become housewives.

Gornick, Vivian and Moran, Barbara K., eds. *Woman in Sexist Society*. New York: New American Library, 1971 (paperback)—essays by modern feminists on the role of women in society.

Hays, H. R. *The Dangerous Sex: The Myth of Feminine Evil*. New York: Pocket Books, 1965 (paperback)—men's fear of women historically.

Komisar, Lucy. *The New Feminism*. New York: Warner, 1972 (paperback)—excellent, informative book on feminism for young people.

Lessing, Doris. *The Golden Notebook*. New York: Ballantine, 1968 (paperback)—novel about a woman writer and her struggle for fulfillment.

Mead, Margaret. *Male and Female*. New York: Dell, 1968 (paperback)—study of cultures around the world with emphasis on the fact that sex roles differ from one society to the next and are therefore not innate characteristics.

Millet, Kate. *Sexual Politics*. Garden City: Doubleday, 1970 —the subjugation of women, especially as illustrated in literature. Difficult but informative reading.

New York City' Commission on Human Rights Report. *Women's Role in Contemporary Society*. New York: Avon, 1972 (paperback)—testimony by great feminists given during the hearings of the commission, on the discrimination against women in our society.

Nin, Anaïs. *Ladders to Fire*. Chicago: Swallow, 1959 (paperback)—novel about a woman who rejects the traditional "feminine" role.

Morgan, Elaine. *The Descent of Woman*. New York: Stein and Day, 1972—the reinterpretation of evolution in the light of the female sex, exploding a great many man-made myths about the history of the human race.

Morgan, Robin, ed. *Sisterhood is Powerful.* New York: Vintage, 1970 (paperback)—writings from the feminist movement.

Woolf, Virginia. *A Room of One's Own.* New York: Harcourt, Brace, 1929—an exquisite essay by the great woman writer on the difficulties all women face in trying to achieve in the professional world.